To

From

GOLF
The Major
Championships
1987

GOLF
The Major Championships 1987

Photography by

PHIL SHELDON

Written by

DAVID AND PATRICIA DAVIES

PARTRIDGE PRESS

TO MY FATHER

I would like to thank the following for their help
in the production of this book: Jan Traylen,
Trevor Jones and Hugh Routledge

Photographs copyright © 1987 by Phil Sheldon
Text copyright © 1987 by David and Patricia Davies

Published in Great Britain by
Partridge Press, Maxwelton House, Boltro Road, Haywards Heath, West Sussex
(Partridge Press is an imprint of Transworld Publishers Ltd, 61-63 Uxbridge Road, London W5)

Designed by Jo Laws

Typeset by BSC Print Ltd, London SW18
Reproduced and Proofed by East Anglian Engraving Co. Ltd, Norwich
Printed and Bound in Great Britain by
W.S. Cowell Ltd, Ipswich

ISBN 1-85225-047-X

CONTENTS
The Majors 1987

THE U.S. MASTERS   6
Augusta National Golf Club, Augusta, Georgia
9-12 April

THE U.S. OPEN   34
Olympic Golf Club, San Francisco, California
18-21 June

THE OPEN   62
Muirfield, Scotland
16-19 July

THE U.S. P.G.A.   90
PGA National, Palm Beach Gardens, Florida
6-9 August

Final Scores   118

The traditional Masters Green Jacket presentation from the 1986 Champion Jack Nicklaus.

THE U.S. MASTERS

AUGUSTA NATIONAL GOLF CLUB, AUGUSTA, GEORGIA

9-12 APRIL

The silence, in Amen Corner, was as intense as in any Cathedral. Larry Hogan Mize was standing over an almost impossible chip to the 11th green of the Augusta National Golf Club. He was faced with 30 yards of clinging rye grass and 10 yards of lightning fast green, knowing that to get down in two from there would be a wonderful achievement. Mize, Augusta born, was about to lose the U.S. Masters at the second hole of a sudden-death play-off.

He hit the chip, hands ahead of the club face, punching down on it, keeping the ball low so that it would bend the rye grass to its will rather than the reverse. The ball bounced twice, hopped onto the green and started rolling quickly, perhaps too quickly, towards the hole. Greg Norman, the surviving member of a play-off trio that had started at the 10th and had included Severiano Ballesteros, watched intently, trying to gauge the pace of the green from his opponent's shot. He had a 30-footer on roughly the same line and wanted all the help he could get.

Mize's chip rolled on, hardly seeming to slow down at all. How far from the pin would it come to rest? But up in the congregation, in the packed spectator mounds that give a view of Amen Corner – the 11th, 12th and 13th holes

– there was a sudden stirring. The ball was on line and, as it got closer, the stirring changed into a crescendo, an outpouring of emotion for a local lad who was being willed, fervently and noisily, to make good.

Mize's ball hit the hole dead centre; it fell in, and in that split second the crescendo of expectation culminated in an explosion of joy. Amen Corner was delirious. Larry Mize, literally the boy from next door, the boy who, 11 years before, had won the Augusta Country Club Junior Championship on the course that runs behind the Corner, had just won the U.S. Masters Championship.

Before Norman had a chance to putt to try to take the play-off to another hole, Mize erupted. Having stood stock still for a second while the enormity of what he had done registered, Mize then took off on a glory run, both arms punching the air above his head. He was exalted, almost overcome. But then, as he ran, he remembered his Christianity. He paused, raised his eyes heavenwards, lifted his hands as if in prayer and then clapped them, as if to applaud the deity for his benificence.

As all this was going on Norman was surveying a putt that had just become virtually impossible. As he did so he had to try to fight back thoughts, inevitable yet truly destructive thoughts, of the last major championship in which he had played, the U.S. P.G.A. in August 1986. On the last hole of the last round Bob Tway, after playing his approach really badly, had hit a bunker shot straight into the cup to take a title that had looked to belong to the Australian. Now Mize had chipped in. Why me, God? Why me?

Such thoughts had to be discarded if the putt were to go in, and Norman shaded his eyes as he hunched over the ball, looking at the line. But, in truth, the putt was never anywhere near. It was always too far left, always too strong, always going to leave him runner-up for the second consecutive major championship.

Norman put a brave face on it. Few men, with the possible exceptions of Ballesteros and Nicklaus, have been asked to deal with such a double disappointment in so short a space of time. It required all the Australian's sportsmanship – and he is not short of that – to congratulate Mize. Afterwards he could not remember what he said. "I wasn't sure I could speak at all, and I'm sure he couldn't," said Norman.

What made the whole thing worse for Norman was the way the two men had played the 11th hole. Norman had driven the ball about 310 yards, well ahead of Mize and it was the Augustan who was first to play. Years ago Ben Hogan said of this second shot: "If ever you see me on the 11th green in two you will know I've hit a bad shot," meaning that the pond on the left was such a dire penalty that he played deliberately out to the right. But not as far to the right as Mize went. As he hit his five-iron Mize instantly turned away from it and murmered: "Oh, my gosh." It was a rank bad shot which must have given instant comfort to Norman. "As soon as I saw it," said Norman, "I said to my caddie: 'I'm going to be right of the flag and get down in two from there'." The unspoken assumption was that Mize could not do similarly from where he was.

Norman's shot fulfilled his intentions. It came to rest on the right edge of the green, safe, a certain four and an almost certain win.

At that moment Mize began to think positively. "In situations like that you have to believe that you're going to make every shot. It helped that in the final round I hit the ball onto the precise line that the chip would have to take once it got onto the green, and I had holed a 12-footer for a birdie." In fact that birdie was a large part of the reason that Mize was again at the 11th hole. It had inspired him to birdie the other Amen Corner holes, to go to four-under-par for the Championship and to get into the play-off.

But his father, Charlie, was less optimistic. "When I saw that second shot," he confessed "I began to pray that he'd get down in just two more." A few long minutes later and Charlie Mize "jumped just as high as I could jump, hollered just as loud as I could holler." His son had not just survived a play-off against the two best golfers in the world, he had beaten them. Ballesteros was already in the club house, having three-putted the 10th from 20 feet. He had departed in tears of frustration, walking up the hill in solitary desolation.

Mize had played the 10th far better than either of the two others. He hit the best, and longest drive; the best and closest second and came within 2 inches of holing the birdie putt. Norman, by contrast, had run through the green, had an 18 foot putt from the fringe and had to hole from just under 3 feet for his par. It might have been easier for Norman had Mize won there and then, but that would have robbed the occasion of some delicious ironies.

In his early years Mize, a golfer of considerable promise growing up in Augusta, had many opportunities to play, as an invited guest, at Augusta National. But he turned them down. "I wanted to earn my way onto the course. I wanted to play there as of right." Instead he played at the Augusta Country Club, the course that borders onto the back of the 12th green and 13th tee. "I used to peek through the fence and look at Amen Corner," said Mize. "I used to

The agony of Greg Norman's missed birdie putt for outright victory at the 72nd hole.

fantasize about winning the Masters." By craning his neck at that fence, Mize would have been able to see the very spot from which, years later, he would fulfil that fantasy.

And fantasy it was. Both men admitted it. Norman said that Mize "could stand there three days and not make that chip again." Mize made it more: "I could hit it a million times and it wouldn't go in again."

Norman was then asked if he could compare Mize's chip with Tway's bunker shot, which is rather like asking a man to make a comparison between a hotel fire and a plane crash. Norman, with familiar charm, made every effort to be patient. but not before he had asked, humorously, for the interview room to be cleared of women members of the press because what he had to say was fit neither for their ears nor for printing. More soberly, he estimated that Mize's shot was 30 per cent more difficult than Tway's because of the distance and the difference in surfaces.

The moment the chip dropped, Mize also dropped one of the cruellest nicknames in golf. Since winning the 1983 Memphis Classic

Mize had led four tournaments, including the 1986 Tournament Players' Championship, but had lost them all badly. He had become known as Larry 'De-Mize', a choker by another name. Because of that, when the play-off started, he was hardly even third favourite. Most people thought Ballesteros would win and those that didn't thought Norman would. Mize was just along for the ride.

But the Augustan felt that he had been badly done by. "Sure I had hit some bad shots under pressure. I have to live with that. But some guys went over the top about me choking. I also had some bad breaks in those situations and those never got mentioned. This time I had a good break. Let's face it, if you live in the past, the present isn't going to be very good."

But now the present is going to be very, very good for Larry Mize. As Jack Nicklaus, no less, the defending champion, slipped the Green Coat around his shoulders, he told him of the doors it would open, of the new life that awaited him as Masters Champion. It was, for Larry Mize, a re-birth and a re-awakening. It was, truly, a miracle at Amen Corner.

◆   JUST THE TICKET

It is impossible to get into the U.S. Masters. Everyone knows that. They stopped selling tickets for the tournament proper, at the gate, 20 years ago and it is nearly a decade since anyone got onto the patron's list. It costs only $85 to buy a series ticket which covers all four days; this is rightly regarded as the best value in sport. But it is not much good knowing that when you have not one chance in a million of laying your hands on one.

Or have you? Listen to a telephone conversation overheard on Sunday at Amen Corner, where there are some 'phones under the trees near the refreshment hut. A woman calling her friend was explaining that she had only paid $3 for her ticket but that she had to hand over her driver's licence as security, and that the licence would only be returned to her on return of the

Mize jumps for joy after his winning chip at the second play-off hole.

ticket itself.

Now that may need some explaining, so let us turn to Larry Cole, from North Carolina. He does not pay any attention to all that negative publicity about tickets. He had been on business in Atlanta and he, and a friend, drove to Augusta to see if they could get into the 1987 Masters on the Friday. Madness, you may think. But they got in, and all it cost them was the $5 they had to pay to park their car in one of the temporary parking lots that spring up in gardens all around the Augusta National during Master's week.

"We got in," Cole explained, "because the guy who parks these cars operates like a broker service. People with badges will come here to park and, if they come out a little early, he will take their badges from them and rent them for the rest of the day to someone else. I've been a fan of golf for some 20 years and I just wanted to see the course – you can see the

Once a Masters patron, always a Masters patron. . . . .

players at other tournaments. We got in about 4 pm, saw the leaders play the last three or four holes, and then walked the back nine."

The next day, Saturday, Cole wanted to see the front nine, but he was having no luck. "Saturday's real popular, but they say there'll be no problem Sunday. I guess a lot of people have to head on back to wherever they're from."

Cole, who had been patrolling up and down near one of the entrance gates to the Club looking for tickets, said the cheapest he had seen go for Saturday and Sunday had been $150 for the two days. "Mind you," he grinned, "it's better value than the agencies. They wanted $1300 for an $85 pass."

Cole eventually struck lucky when he met a man we can call 'Jim'. Jim, and his wife Elizabeth advise everyone to avoid the touts, the 'scalpers' as they call them. "When someone's asking an outrageous amount, shy away from them because that's not necessary," says Elizabeth. "No need to pay $1500; perhaps $25 or $35 for the day, or maybe $70 if the tournament's tight."

Jim, an ebullient man who rarely stands still, does not have a scale of charges. "If someone wants to pay $5 I wait until I find them a ticket for $5. If they say they'll pay $500 then if someone comes up and wants $500 for their ticket I know I've got a person who'll buy it. If there's not a customer then I don't buy the ticket; I just let it go."

He rarely deals in very large sums, reckoning to make just $300 over the four days. "I make offa four days of hassle what one scalper makes offa one ticket," he laughs, "but it's an accommodation thing and I love it."

His car parking makes him about $1500 but, as he is a successful businessman anyway, the principal reason for doing it is the friends he has made who come back year after year. "Patrons who rent their badges out like to deal with someone they can trust, someone who will get their tickets back to them. Every ticket has a number and Augusta National has a list of

the numbers with the names to which they belong. So the patrons have to get them back. Like Thursday, I had 17 tickets and every one of them had to be back in the person's hand that night. And then Friday, because I had held up my side, I had nine tickets for Friday. Saturday I've had three. Tomorrow, Sunday, I could probably have 50.

"The ones for Sunday, see, they won't have to have 'em back. Though I do have some people I have to mail 'em back to. They want their badge. They want that same number back, to know that it's safe, that it didn't get pulled. Because, if it gets pulled, it's over, it's forever."

Jim's brokerage has so far survived any threats from the law. "I feel that there was a girl that came by here one year that was a police officer and she was trying to get me to sell her a ticket. But I don't sell tickets, I just rent them on a daily basis. I call it 'flip-flops', 'cos that's all I do – I flip the ticket over there, then it flops back up over here."

That is the essence of Jim's operation – you go on spec. If there is a ticket, well and good. If not, just sit on down here, drink a few beers, eat some pizza, have a few laughs. You can always watch golf on the telly!

Past Masters. Sam Snead (1949, 1952, 1954), Gene Sarazen (1935) and Byron Nelson (1937, 1942) tee off in a pre-tournament exhibition match. Below, Arnold Palmer (1958, 1960, 1962, 1964) who missed the cut in 1987.

◆ A CHAMPION OVERLOOKED

One of the older Augusta traditions is that most fatuous of exercises, the pre-picking of the winner. The local paper asks a selection of club professionals and golf correspondents to nominate the man who, at the end of the week, will have won the first major championship of the season. The only surprise is that so many agree to do so. Golf is not a game that lends itself to predictions; not only are there all the complexities of human form and nature, but there is the game itself, surely the most complex of sports. So how do the pundits fare? Ray Floyd won in 1976 with a record-equalling total, without a single vote being cast for him to finish in the first three. And, almost needless to say, despite the fact of his being a home-town boy, the same thing happened to Larry Mize in 1987.

The 28-year-old Augustan was, despite his success in terms of money won – $988 342 before the Championship started – a fairly anonymous figure. There has never been a great deal of glamour attached to Larry Mize, who is content to pull down his visor over his eyes, cloak his emotions and be very careful off the course not to cause any controversy. All that, combined with the fact that he was perceived as a money-maker rather than as a tournament winner, made him easy to disregard. And disregarded he was. Even in his home town, even playing the Masters and even, during the first round, when he should have been on the leader-board, Mize was overlooked.

He had opened up with a two-under-par 70 which, on that first day, was a superb score. With glassy greens aligned with a firm surface the pros found themselves shooting off the putting surface and into places from whence it was impossible to get down in two more. There was a lot of bleating about it and even Bernhard Langer, whose 71 was only two behind the leader, John Cook, called the greens unfair. It was impossible, Langer said, to hit a three-wood onto them and be sure of it

John Cook led the first round with a 69.

Corey Pavin and Payne Stewart (opposite) both shot 71 on the first day.

staying on the putting surface. It is, of course, debatable as to whether you *should* be able to do that, but the Augusta authorities had decreed that you would not be able to and some players, like Tom Watson and Jack Niclaus, agreed with them.

Mize was not even asked for his opinion, and for most of the day hardly anyone, press or public, knew that he was playing so well. His name was not put up on the huge leaderboards that dot the course, and which, on that first day, charted the progress of such notable characters as Buddy Alexander and David Curry, the respective American and British

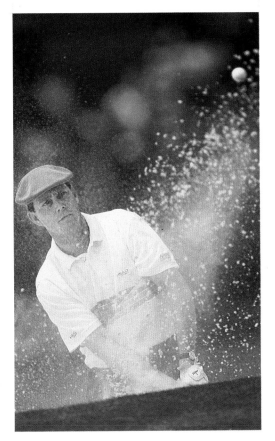

amateur champions. The fact was that Mize was only level-par for most of the day; it was not until he suddenly birdied the last two holes that he found himself in sole possession of second place.

The leader-board system had to do something about it and, belatedly, they put up a kind of coded message in the space that they keep for urgent messages to the public. It read 'Mize 2. 18,' which, for those in the know, meant that he was two-under at the end of the round. Typically, Mize was unimpressed. "Well, it was a kinda so-so round, I suppose," he said, "and then – boom!"

'So-so' or not, it had its significance. In the last round of the 1986 Masters Mize had scored a 65 and it was clear that the course, far from holding any terrors for him, was actually very much to his liking. He had played well in that 65, not so in the 70. "I saved par with pretty good putts at three holes," he said. "I guess I just scraped it around when I had to."

Modest to a fault, you may think, and the sort of remark that led to a devastating summation of Mize when he went on to win. "Well," said an American scribe, "the meek have finally inherited the earth."

Elsewhere there was more debate and division over the greens. Nicklaus was asked about the little shots around the fringes and he recalled Miller Barber's famous remark in 1966, the last time the greens were in a similar condition. "It's like," said Barber, "trying to putt from a haystack onto a highway." Sandy Lyle, on the other hand (and on the back of a 77), said they were a joke. They were, he said, in danger of 'burning up'; indeed, if some of Lyle's glares at them had lasted a second or two longer there might have been spontaneous combustion.

Ballesteros and Norman, both with scores of 73 to be joint 14th, accepted what they found. They were probably playing the Gary Player mind-game which says that you must always think that the course on which you are currently playing, and the greens on which you are currently putting, are the finest on earth.

◆ THE SECOND DAY

In any championship the winner usually plays a bad round and gets away with it. It could be said that the definition of a really good player is one who plays a round that deserves a 76 and returns a 72. That is what Mize did on Friday.

He admitted it. "I struggled more than I like to and I'm happy to get out of it with a 72. Everyone hits bad shots but I hit more than I care to today, so I feel happy to have scratched it around." This is the man, remember, who 'scraped it around' on Thursday.

The effort left Mize almost totally exhausted. "I just couldn't relax out there. I feel I've played 36 holes. If you don't play well this Augusta course will get you, just wear you out."

But Mize, at two-under-par, was only one shot behind Curtis Strange and the leader board, at this stage, was not the classic sight it was to become later. Jack Nicklaus, five behind, said: "There are not the names up there that there were last year. I've got to shoot 69, 65, something like that, but if I get a few putts rolling, I don't see why I can't be in contention."

Among the 'names' that Nicklaus had in mind were Ballesteros, who was joint 9th, Norman, joint 23rd and Crenshaw, joint 13th. The latter was surely doing all he could to hex himself out of it. Not only was he now 13th, he had, on Wednesday, won the Par Three contest and no-one, in the history of the Masters, had ever won on both the big and the small course in the same week. Crenshaw had come to the last hole of the Par Three in a winning position only to be urged by his father to hit his tee shot into the water. But he couldn't, wouldn't, do it and paid the price – if we are to believe the superstition.

The Par Three had something else special in 1987. Mac O'Grady played the course left-handed. He is naturally ambidextrous and scored a respectable two-over-par 29. He is also naturally eccentric and, in December 1986, had asked the P.G.A. Tour if they would

Ambidextrous Mac O'Grady played the Par Three tournament left handed.

let him compete in the Chrysler Team Championship as a one-man team, playing two balls, one as a left-hander and one as a right-hander. "They just said 'no'," said O'Grady, "can you believe it?"

To the naked eye, O'Grady's two swings are strikingly similar. "Yes," says O'Grady, "the swings are pretty close. But it's one thing to move the club in the same geometry, quite another to fine-tune the motor neurons." Quite.

Back on the big course Howard Clark, in his first Masters after being misguidedly left uninvited for the previous two years, was lying joint 13th with rounds of 74 and 71. He was playing well and, on the lightning greens, putting wonderfully. In the second round he completed the first nine holes with only ten putts, with eight singles, and made the cut with six shots

Europeans who missed the cut: amateurs Garth McGimpsey and David Curry, and (above) José Maria Olazabal who finished second on the 1986 PGA European Tour Order of Merit.

to spare. Langer was joint fifth, having eagled the 15th and rescued a bogey at the 16th after finding the water with his tee shot. Norman was totally out of sorts and Ballesteros was not too happy either. At the long 8th, going for a big drive, he hooked hopelessly and the ball, going left, hit a tree and went deep into the forest, further to the left. The only way out was onto the 2nd fairway. He hit a four-iron out of the trees to the top of the hill. Then he hit another four-iron, blind, 175 yards over the intervening jungle. This fell just short of the green and, with a huge hump between him and the pin, he chipped and took six.

On his trudge up the 2nd fairway he met the last group coming down. "Oh yes," said Seve "I was able to say 'hello' to Larry." When he got in, he said something else, very un-Seve-like. "I try to play the first three rounds very carefully, so that I have a chance to win." Let us hope that he never forgets that when he won the Masters in 1980 he started with a 66 and, in 1983, with a 68.

The leader, Strange, was unwittingly kind to a group of nine golfers on 151, a score distinctly on the high side for making the cut. The record low is 145 in 1979, the high is 154 in 1982 and all Strange had to do to put out the nine was hole from 2½ feet at the 17th, or from 10 feet at the 18th. He missed both putts and, among others, Sandy Lyle survived. So did Bob Lewis, to take automatically the amateur medal, but there were some distinguished casualties. Lee Trevino, Ray Floyd, Hal Sutton and Bob Tway of the fancied candidates took the early plane and the European contingent was thinned by the loss of José Maria Olazabal, David Curry and Garth McGimpsey.

◆ ALL-CHANGE DAY

Saturday is all-change day. The day that those who will, do; those who might have, haven't. The leader-board at the end of Saturday was one of the best in recent memory, chock full of names that count, of men who could and, for the most part, already had. Four of the leading eight players were major championship winners, four of the eight were Americans, four of the eight were 'forners', as anyone from outside the States gets called. One of the latter category, Greg Norman, said: "We've got a good pot boiling." Jack Nicklaus commented: "There's a lot of cream on the leader-board now," adding that, in his opinion, Norman was the man who "realistically everyone now has to beat." The board read:

212 Crenshaw, Maltbie
213 Langer, Norman
214 Ballesteros, Chen, Mize, Strange.

The best round of the day belonged to Norman, a 66 that moved him from three-over-par to three-under, and that put fear into the rest of the field. But the Australian had needed to work not just on his shots but also on his mental attitude. "I had been trying too hard," said Norman, "and it had an inhibiting effect on my game. But after that 74 I told myself: 'Hey, this is silly. You know you can play here. You like the course, go out and enjoy it.' So I went out and I charged more putts, I played more aggressively and I managed to do it without making any rash mistakes."

Norman's inhibitions may have been a result of the way he threw the tournament away in 1986. But also, it must be remembered, he wanted to win the Masters like no other major except, perhaps, the British Open. "I love this place," he said, "I have an affinity for it." There was, however, an interesting, and literal, straw in the wind when Norman played the 11th. As he approached the tee he glanced up at his name on the leader-board; he did so at the precise moment that the breeze tugged at the letters of his name and whole lot, from 'N' to 'N', tumbled from the hoarding. "I just hope," he said "that I don't fall off the leader-board going through Amen Corner." He didn't – not then, at any rate.

The wind made it a difficult day and, although he hardly overpowers the ball, Ben Crenshaw is one of the best wind players at Augusta. The reason is experience. Crenshaw has played 15 Masters, and by knowing how the wind was going to behave, was able to get round in 67, giving himself the best possible chance of defying superstition. Dave McNeilly, long-time caddie for Nick Faldo, tells how Crenshaw frequently waits for just the right moment to hit the ball: "In '84, the year he won, we were on the 5th tee and we must have stood there for nearly two minutes, waiting for a particular gust of wind to come up. He'd worked out in his mind where it should be coming from and all the while that it was blowing in his face he was just waiting and waiting. Then, when it stopped swirling, he went ahead

1986 Masters Champion Jack Nicklaus with his son as caddy finished joint seventh.

Severiano Ballesteros with his brother as caddy attending *behind* the flag in Seve's new ploy to block out distractions in his line of sight.

and hit his shot." Crenshaw's 67, with five birdies on the last nine, left him, once again, the man all America looked to to repel the 'forners'.

He was joined, at the end of the day, by Roger Maltbie, a man whom no-one expected to win. Back in 1975 Maltbie was a rookie. But he was a talented rookie and, by virtue of a little luck, won back-to-back tournaments. The game was evidently easy and Maltbie was never slow to celebrate that fact. His second winner's cheque, for $40 000, was left in a bar, and still hangs on the wall behind the beer pumps.

But three years later he was 129th on the Tour Money List, the next year 155th and it was not until 1985 he began to re-apply himself. In that year he won two tournaments and, as a mature 35-year-old, was seen as a threat once more, although hardly at this level. He was asked if he would sleep before the final round. "Oh, I'll be okay," he grinned. "Coupla drinks'll do it." Two hours later he was still at the club house bar when the British press assembled for their annual Saturday night party. Maltbie threatened to join in, "I'm half British anyway," said the man whose mother is from Scotland. Maltbie represents an American brewers called Michelob. He has their name on his visor and all over his bag; the company's slogan, repeated incessantly over the airwaves, is: "The night belongs to Michelob." Nice man though he is, it seemed certain that the next day would not belong to Roger Maltbie.

Bernhard Langer, the 1985 Master, had begun the week with the usual three putters in his bag for the practice rounds, plus, this time, three wedges as well. Peter Coleman, his caddie, is accustomed to these overloads but, like the rest of us, wishes he did not have to carry them. In Coleman's case it is a simple matter of weight, but everyone else knows that if ever Langer really sorts out his short game then we will have a real champion on our hands. Of the leaders Langer had had by far the most consis-

tent rounds and had seemingly conquered his dislike of the firm greens.

Strangely, of the other leaders, Ballesteros was the next most consistent, despite an appalling record, for him, on the long holes. He was no better than level-par for the tournament at the par-fives, having played 12 of them. Norman, by way of contrast, was five-under for the same holes.

"I make mistakes," he said. "I swing too hard, too fast. I try to hit the ball too hard." On the 13th he almost swung himself off his feet trying to get the ball round the dog-leg to the left; instead he clattered the ball into the trees on the right. He had to play out short of the stream in front of the green, chipped on and saw the ball get to within 15 feet of the pin and then roll back down a bank to finish 40 feet away. From there he three-putted and so, in effect, gave two shots to the field.

While Ballesteros was doing this, a little further ahead, Curtis Strange was getting embarrassed. The 16th green has always been a severe trial and tribulation if you either miss it or finish in the wrong place, that is above the hole. Strange hit a good tee shot that finished 12 feet from the hole and, although it was a downhill putt, elected to go for it. "It just exploded off the putter," said Strange afterwards. The ball ran and ran and, as it trickled some 40 feet past the cup, some people laughed. "It was my fault and I felt silly," said Strange. "There are times out there when the golf course can humble and embarrass you."

It was because of Strange, of course, that Lyle was playing in the third round at all. And he made the most of it. Out in par, he had four successive birdies on the back nine, at the 13th, 14th, 15th and 16th to be back in 32 for a 68 which left him in line for a rather large cheque. Lyle, although trusting his new teacher, Jimmy Ballard from Florida, was having a certain amount of difficulty in putting theory into practice. As this theory involved eliminating one of his lifetime faults, that of sweeping the club back around his right ankle,

Europeans who made the cut. Sandy Lyle finished 17th, Howard Clark 35th.

it was hardly surprising that he sometimes reverted to his former ways.

Since winning the Tournament Players' Championship, Lyle had missed the cut while defending the Greater Greensboro Open and had all but missed the cut at Augusta. There was obviously some consolation work to be done.

Howard Clark was also having his problems. It is difficult to come to Augusta and play well first time round and when you lose your driving, as did Clark, it is impossible. After a promising start, albeit with his putter working overtime, the third round caught up with him and a 40 on the back nine gave him a 77. He was even worse than Seve on the par fives: two-over for the tournament. Still, he was now joint 30th and a place in the top 24 was obviously a possibility.

Meanwhile Larry Mize had his best ball-striking round so far – and yet it still added up to 72.

"My putter was a little cold," he said, and at Augusta that freezes anyone's score. After 12 holes Mize was three-over-par, having three-putted the 4th and 8th holes and gone into the water at the 12th. But he birdied the 13th, 16th and 18th, the latter for the second time in three rounds, and the dreams were beginning to be remembered. "Everyone's expecting Greg or Seve to do it," he said "and no-one's expecting me to do too much. Maybe I can slip right in there. I've dreamed about winning here. I've dreamed about winning coming from behind, winning going away, winning just every way I could."

But for one man the dream was over. Corey Pavin, leading money winner on the U.S. Tour, took 81 to fall back to joint 37th. As he walked off the 18th green his wife, Shannon, walked up to him with their 11-month-old son, Ryan. "I brought you your son," she said. "I figured you needed to see a smiling face."

'Fore right' for Mize's drive at the 8th on Sunday. But it was playing partner Curtis Strange who really strayed, taking 76 to finish joint 15th.

◆ SUNDAY AT THE 18TH

The leaders are not due out until 2.15. The first pair, hardly dewsweepers, will not be teeing off until 10.47. Yet even before 9.00 am, the advance guard of spectators has arrived, laying claim to prime positions at the 18th. They are not allowed to rope their plots off so they do the next best thing. They settle their little tubular steel chairs, with the green canvas seats and the green canvas backs resplendent with white Masters logo, on their chosen site. Then it's off to have breakfast or check out the pin positions, secure in the knowledge that their chairs will still be there when they get back.

Already several rows of chairs are in place and, though the scene is still green and tranquil rather than multi-coloured and restless, a few stalwarts are already installed with their sandwiches, crosswords, binoculars, suntan lotions, raincoats and their weighty Sunday newspapers.

There is activity to the right of the green, as you look down the hill from the club house. A couple of photographers are securing cameras to the scaffolding of the small stand erected to give them an uninterrupted view of the winner's moment of triumph, play-offs permitting.

The Masters is a difficult tournament for the photographers. They are not allowed inside the ropes and things are especially taxing on the last day when they have to keep both a lens on the leaders and an eye on the leader-board – and all this while infiltrating themselves, and their equipment, through the huge crowds that gather round both greens and tees.

To the left of the photographers' stand, behind the green, is the scorer's tent where the players check and sign their cards immediately they finish their round. The tent is also a focal point for Leo Beckmann, a retired golf professional from Savannah who has, for the last 19 years, stood behind the 18th green, resplendent in a bright red blazer,

The 18th green at 8am, with spectators already laying claim to prized positions.

keeping the crowd informed.

"Really you try to give 'em correct information," he says, "confirming a player's score and giving 'em a little run down on each player. They know how to read the leader-board but a lot of them don't bother to do it too much and when you get up to give the scores, they're quiet, very quiet, 'cos they want to hear.

"I give the scores on both sides, but I talk mainly to the left side because if I go on the other side, then I'm projecting right towards the 9th green and I have to watch that. There's a flagman on one of the stands, and if he has the flag up it tells me to keep my big mouth shut, there's somebody putting on the 9th.

"My aim is not to make any mistakes," grins Leo, who has become a bit of a celebrity thanks to his appearances at the Masters. "If you make one, they'll know it because this is a very knowledgeable gallery, they know everything that's going on at the Masters golf tournament, and everything that has gone on."

Leo does not have to scramble for his place on Sunday, he is in no danger of having his view obscured and he appreciates his good fortune: "Here's one of the great sporting events of the world, and here I am out in the middle of the arena at the conclusion. It's the number one position to see the golf tournament."

Ah well, when we feel envious of Leo, we can always think of the play-off.

All morning the pace is deceptively calm and unhurried but there is a tense, expectant atmosphere as everybody, players, caddies, officials, press, photographers and patrons, anticipates the excitement to come. All are keen to play their part to the best of their ability. Larry Mize and his father Charlie have finished packing the car together and discussed his chances of winning. Dad tells Larry to practise his short game and 'hit 'em good'.

Larry tees off at 1.51 and there are thousands upon thousands of people milling around the course by now. There are more rows of chairs at the 18th, many of them occupied by people

Two former Champions who made the cut. Top, Gary Player (1961, 1974, 1978) and (above) finding trouble in Rae's Creek, Tommy Aaron (1973).

Ben Crenshaw and Roger Maltbie were both in contention until the last few holes, but finished one stroke behind the three leaders.

Langer drives off the 18th tee to a disappointing final round 76.

When Mize's second shot at the 15th went through the green, it seemed that his chance of donning the Green Jacket had disappeared into the water along with his ball.

who are simply going to sizzle in the sun for another four or five hours.

By 3.25 the last pair, Ben Crenshaw and Roger Maltbie, are on the fourth, a couple of holes behind Mize and there are 17 rows of chairs banked round the 18th green. Leo apprises the crowd of the fortunes of the early starters and there is generous applause, or sympathetic groaning, as the non-contenders putt out.

If you are not in position by now, you have little chance of seeing all you want to see by the time it is 6.00 – what you are missing right now is Mize playing that little nine-iron into the 18th green. You will be dodging and weaving, jumping and ducking in your efforts to get a glimpse of the green, let alone the pin, through the people standing several rows deep behind the rows of chairs that you know stretch for yards.

The bad news is that Leo Beckmann has no intention of retiring just yet, and the guy who does the announcing on the 9th is in line to take over anyway. So maybe there is something to be said for play-offs after all.

◆   COUNT DOWN TO A PLAY-OFF

Tom Weiskopf, a man of vastly unfulfilled golfing talent, was working for CBS TV during the 1987 Masters. Before the start of play on the last day he announced: "The one who wins will be the one who makes the least mistakes." Not only was he lacking in insight and originality but he was to be hopelessly wrong.

As the day unfolded it became obvious that, of the men who led on the last day, variously, Crenshaw, Maltbie, Mize, Norman and Ballesteros, it was the Spaniard who was playing the most relentless, remorseless and least error-prone golf of the lot. Ballesteros had had, in fact, that kind of week. Head down, low-profile, interviews on the run – a tunnel-vision week with nothing in sight but a Green Coat.

Seve has an elephantine memory, and recalls not only his failure of 1986 but also the

furore that being misquoted at the start of that week caused. "I have come to win the tournament," became "I am going to win the tournament," in the American press. It was to haunt Ballesteros throughout the proceedings that year. So, no chances this time, as shown by his performance on Saturday evening:

"Did you play good today Seve?"

"The ball did not find the hole, but 70 is still a good round."

"Will you be disappointed if you lose on Sunday?"

"You cannot lose anything, only win."

And, most asinine of all, "Who's gonna win, then, Seve?"

"There are many good players on the leader-board and they all play good. I tell you on Sunday night who wins."

That, then, was Seve's mood, and it showed on the course. Mistakes? Of the three men who tied on 285, Ballesteros had 13 pars, Mize had seven and Norman had six in rounds of, respectively, 71, 72 and 71. Looked at in another way, Ballesteros had two bogies, Mize five and Norman six.

This was a grinding and teeth-gritting Ballesteros, totally determined not to make the kind of disastrous mistake he had the previous year. For all the amnesia he had claimed over the 15th in 1986, when a watery four-iron cost him the title, Seve still hears the splash; the ripples still spread through his memory. And so he played par golf. Three birdies, two bogies, and who could beat him in a play-off?

His most uncertain moments had been around Amen Corner when, at the 11th, he missed the green on the right and, not quite in Mize country, played an adequate chip to 12 feet only to miss the putt. He had to hole from 18 feet for his par at the next and went through the green at the 13th, failing, yet again, to get a birdie there. He had to wait until the 17th before a splendidly struck second gave him a five footer which took him to three-under. And to stay on that mark he had to get up and down from the right-hand bunker at the 18th. This put him in the play-off.

At the start of 1987 Norman was playing like Seve used to, just as Seve used to play like Arnie. Norman's driving was transcontinental; his game, at the start of Masters week anyway, transcendental. He shifted from one form of hitting the ball to another, a change that involved moving his nose one inch closer to the ground. This had the effect of lowering both his head and the whole of his upper frame; this, in turn, dropped the hands into a lower position and brought them, the club and the ball, closer to his feet. Try it. It was intended to eliminate the shot that flies to the right; the shot that, in 1986, cost Norman the chance of a play-off with Jack Nicklaus when he came to the 18th needing a par for that opportunity. His second shot flew sharp right into the crowds and Norman did well to take only five.

"If I could have just one shot in my life back again, that'd be the one," said Norman at the start of the week. But his chosen method of eliminating his problem led to an outbreak of awful puns, like getting his nose to the grindstone, stooping to conquer and the nose (no's) having it.

His final round fluctuated madly. Three-under to start with, he was four-under after five, dropped shots at each of the next two holes and then missed a simple 6 foot birdie at the 9th.

Worse was to follow. Through the green at the 10th, three putts at the 11th, missing from only 5 feet, and Norman was back to level par; at that point he was lying three behind Crenshaw, two behind Maltbie, Mize and Langer and one behind Ballesteros. He was seemingly out of it, exactly as he had been in 1986 when he took six at the 10th. But just as he did then, Norman began to play better once the immediate pressure was off. With the best tee shot of the final round at the short 12th, hit to within 6 feet, he got a stroke back. The 13th is no more than a five- or six-iron second for Norman if he gets his drive away and that was

him back to two-under-par and suddenly he was back into the tournament as joint leader with Crenshaw once the latter had birdied the 15th, getting on in two.

Not that it was over yet. A poor club pick at the 16th saw him over the green, from whence it was impossible to get down in two and he duly ran the ball 20 feet past the hole. Two-under, and up ahead Mize was on the 18th, preparing his 4-footer that would take him to three-under. Under the ultimate sword of needing a birdie to have at least the chance of a play-off, Norman hit his second to within 30 feet on the 17th, holed it and walked off the green, putter aloft, as if he had known all along that it would go in.

In fact he almost obviated the need for a play-off. At the 18th, far from pushing his tee shot, he hit it 305 yards, hooking, so that it finished among the spectators, under a trash can. It was only 100 yards to the green. He hit it to 18 feet and how the putt stayed out Norman, and thousands of others, will never know.

So then there were three: Mize, Norman and Ballesteros, all three-under, while on the 17th Crenshaw, who had been three-under most of the day, was going through the green, chipping down to 5 feet, missing the putt and missing the play-off.

Mize's round had been almost equally roller-coaster. Three birdies and two bogies on the front nine got him out in 35 and a birdie at the 13th took him to four-under-par. He was, at that point, the tournament leader, but it has to be admitted, no-one got overly excited about this. Wasn't he Larry De-Mize, the choker? The same man who had five bogies in the last six holes of the 1986 Tournament Players' Championship to lose a four shot lead over John Mahaffey. The same man who had led four tournaments since the last time he had won, and thrown them all away. So there was no need to worry about good ol' Larry, was there?

No there wasn't. No sooner had he gone into

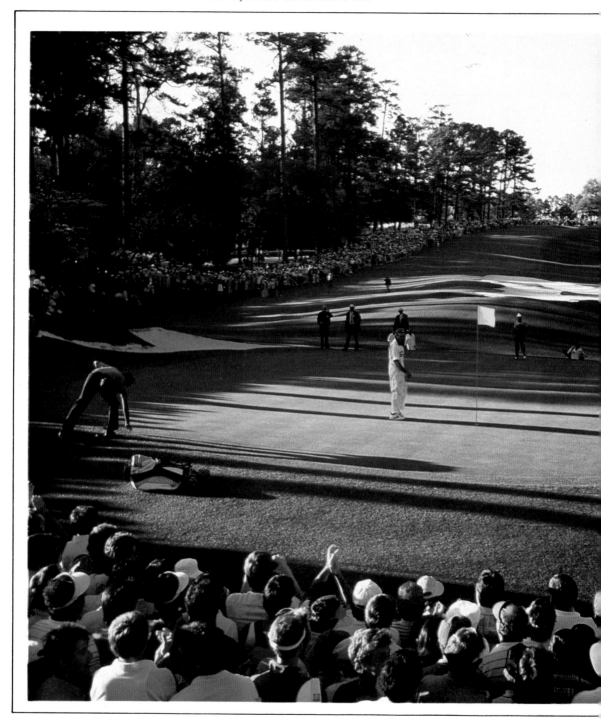

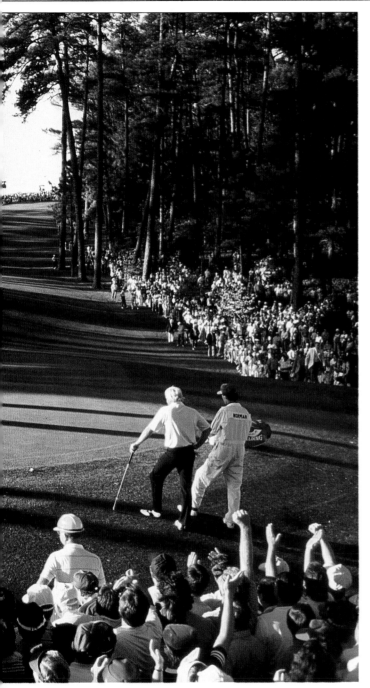

Lengthening shadows heighten the drama at the first play-off hole.

Happy families. An unforgettable moment for Bonnie, Larry and David Mize.

the lead then he began to reverse. He over hit the 14th green, finishing on top of a knoll at the back. The only place he could go from there was at least 8 feet past the pin – and back to three-under-par. Then Mize hit his second, at the 15th, over the green and, as it trickled down to the pond that forms the hazard for the 16th, the sniggers started in earnest. This was choking in its grandest form.

Mize had to drop out under penalty and then he mishit his chip to the green and was short in four. The seven that now stared him in the face was overcome by a lovely little chip down the slope, but it was still a six; surely now we could turn our attention to the real players, the ones who, like thoroughbreds, responded when the going got tough. So it was that Mize got two solid pars at the following two holes and the next thing the world in general knew about him was the roar that greeted his second to the 18th.

Mize stood there, in the middle of the fairway, for what seemed an age, having an argument with his caddie. Mize, the adrenalin flowing, wanted to take a nine-iron for the remaining 120 yards. His caddie knew it was the eight. But in winning the argument, Mize won the championship. He hit the nine, knowing that in the circumstances it would fly further than usual, and he hit it absolutely flush. It carried high over the front bunker, over the pin and over the level part of the green where the flag was, pitching perfectly into the bank that forms the barrier to the upper part of the green.

Then, just as Mize knew it would, the ball started trickling slowly back towards the hole and to the massive, concerted urgings of the huge crowds, slithered down the slope to within 5, maybe 4, feet. It was a magnificent shot, hit under extreme pressure.

Suddenly perceptions began to change. Anyone who could hit that kind of shot, in front of thousands of his home-town folks, knowing that he had to if he was to have any chance of winning the one championship above all others that he had desired since childhood,

surely such a man could not miss the birdie putt?

Mize holed it, confidently too, and punched the air for the first time that day. He was the leader in the club house; let the others catch him if they could.

It was some 45 minutes later that sports' editors throughout the length and breadth of Britain were found having spasms. The play-off hadn't started and, with the 5-hour time difference between the East coast of America and the UK, deadline times were stretched and broken. But it was all deemed to be worthwhile, for wasn't one of the two greatest golfers in the world about to win the Masters? But midnight was approaching, and every second counted and the golfers, heedless of the hacks, were selfishly scrutinising every mortal thing plus, as Damon Runyan would have it, 'and then some'.

The writers, to save those precious seconds, began to sketch out their stories. To hell with natural sympathies, Seve departing at the 10th only made the story simpler. Now we could, and I did, write: 'Greg Norman, the Great White Shark who was floundering in the shallows after 11 holes, surfaced superbly to win a sudden-death play-off for the U.S. Masters Championship at Augusta National golf club yesterday. . .' More in equity than expectation, I also wrote: 'Larry Mize, middle-name Hogan, washed away one of the cruellest jibes in sport when he won the U.S. Masters at Augusta National golf club yesterday. In a sudden-death play-off he beat the two best golfers in the world and, in so doing, stifled the critics who had called him Larry De-Mize. . .'

The first story, of course, got no further than the bin beside the typewriter; the second surely astonished those few breakfast tables it found its way on to. Larry Mize, who only seven years ago was earning a living by picking up balls at a driving range, had won the U.S. Masters, and both Severiano Ballesteros and Greg Norman had to say Amen to that ●

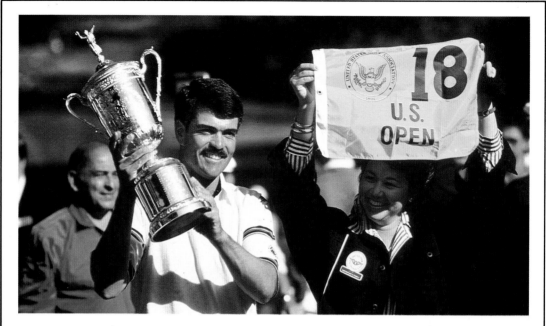

The official, and unofficial, US Open trophy held aloft by Scott and Cheryl Simpson.

Victory in sight for Scott Simpson at the 72nd hole.

THE U.S. OPEN

OLYMPIC GOLF CLUB, SAN FRANCISCO, CALIFORNIA

18-21 JUNE

The words echoed resoundingly around the huge room. On the eve of the U.S. Open Championship the United States Golf Association and 300 guests were honouring Tom Watson by giving him the Bobby Jones Award for 'distinguished services to sportsmanship in golf'. They were making a good job of it too.

Byron Nelson, friend and mentor, and a man who once won 11 PGA tournaments in a row said: "Knowing Tom Watson has been one of the great things in my life. If Bobby Jones were alive, he would agree 100 per cent with this award."

Sandy Tatum, friend and former President of the USGA said: "I once played at Royal Dornoch, in Scotland, with Tom. It was blowing a gale and pouring with rain and yet it was a joy to be on the course with him. Then, after a drink, when it was raining and blowing even harder, we went out again. And do you know, I've never had more fun in my life."

There were glowing tributes to a man who has not only won eight major championships and 31 tournaments on the US Tour, but who has also graced the game worldwide throughout a 16-year professional career. But they were tributes to a man who won the last of the majors in 1983, and the last of the tournaments

in 1984 and, whilst they were obviously not intended as such, the words began to sound ominously like an obituary to a career that was over.

Watson, even if the thought had occurred to him, said nothing. He made a gracious acceptance speech, recalling some of the great moments of his career, detailing some of the great courses – Dornoch, St Andrews, Ballybunion, Pebble Beach, Cypress Point and Augusta National – that he had played, and then mentioned the best celebration he had ever experienced. "Having won the Open Championship at Turnberry in 1977, after that unbelievable battle with Jack Nicklaus, I went back to the Turnberry Hotel to my room. After a few moments a lone piper struck up outside on the lawn. It was all too much. I cried."

It was a poignant moment in that big room in San Francisco, but there was no sadness in Watson's voice. In fact it was clear from his attitude, his tone of voice, his general demeanour, that an obituary was out of place. As he sat down the room rose to give him a standing ovation. If anything rekindled the competitive fires in Tom Watson that week, the Bobby Jones Award Dinner surely did so. The next day Watson went out onto the Olympic Club's Lake course and began the process that was so nearly to end in victory.

He was, at the finish, deservedly beaten by an outstanding performance from Scott Simpson. But Tom Watson was Tom Watson again, and that was as important as anything which emerged from the 87th U.S. Open Championship.

◆ THE OLYMPIC CLUB, SAN FRANCISCO

It is 17 years since Dave Hill flounced out of the U.S. Open at Chaksa, Minnesota, claiming that the course should be given back to the cows. Hill, of course, was given to the wild pronouncement, not to mention the odd bout of club-chucking, and no-one took him all that seriously.

Many people since Hill have, in fact, criticised U.S. Open courses and, because of the often inordinate length of the rough, have allowed mention of cows to creep into the conversation.

But the Olympic Club course was not one that was widely reviled. The grass was long and penal, but mostly in places where you shouldn't be anyway, and despite the fact that the site has a lovely bit of history to it, involving the animal that William McGonagall described so shatteringly accurately as being:

    a creature all forlorner.
    It stands in the rain
    With a leg at each corner,
no-one, this year, mentioned cows.

Bill Callan is the club historian and he it was who revealed that American capitalism, mixed in with a bit of bartering, was alive and well on the site of the Olympic Club courses in the early 1800's. The whole area was bought, in 1835, for the sum of $4 and then, in 1837, sold for $25 and 100 cows. It first became a golf course in 1917 and the current owners bought it a year later. It has always had two courses on the site but one of the originals, which ran down to the Pacific, vanished in the winter storms of 1925 and 1926, which was when the course used for this year's Championship came into being.

At that time it was treeless and had huge greens. Now it looks as if it has been carved out of a forest and has tiny greens.

Callan says: "The trees were planted to protect the members. It can blow pretty fiercely here. And the greens were reduced in size during the Depression years – it was cheaper to maintain smaller greens and they have just stayed that way."

Callan was a three-handicapper before he became involved in research about the club's history and has now gone up to six. Nevertheless he accurately described the effect that the Lake course at Olympic has on a player.

"Most of these guys don't play these kinds of courses but sure, they can get by for a couple of days. But it's up and down and sloping, you never get a flat lie. There's no water, no place for a big swing of strokes, but all of a sudden you miss a coupla fairways and the trees start to enclose. That tree-line begins to get oppressive and, all of a sudden, all you're seeing is rough."

The planning for the Open took over two years and ultimately involved some 1600 volunteers. "They work their tails off," said Callan. "Some of them start at 6.00am and go on until 10.00 at night, in some cases all week. We've got people in their 70's working until 1.30 in the morning."

It has long been a feature of the U.S. Open that the marshalling of the 18 holes is allocated, hole-by-hole, to clubs in the vicinity, who provide complete teams to do it. Every year the marshalls are asked to dress in uniform so that the crowd can readily distinguish them, and they are even asked to pay for the uniform themselves.

"We took a committee decision this year," says Callan "and there were mixed feelings about the style of the uniform."

There certainly were. The uniform consisted of red and beige Argyll socks, beige plus-fours, a red and beige sweater and a beige flat hat, Hogan style. It was a bit like having a thousand reincarnations of Scott Fitzgerald wandering over the premises, and one marshall so disliked the gear that he refused to travel to the course in it, carrying it instead in a plastic bag and changing on arrival.

However, from a marshalling point of view it was, like it or not, an outstanding success. Everyone knew who was a marshall and who was not, if only because people realised that no-one would dress up like that unless they had to. And everyone who did so paid £80 of their own money for the privilege.

Happily the Olympic is one of the less stuffy of American country clubs. There are over 1000 golfing members and altogether, including the city-centre Olympic Club, there are around 8000 members. There is a £1500 joining fee and if you want to play golf there is an additional £7500 to be paid. Additionally there is about £125 per month for green fees etc. and so, while it is not cheap, it's not expensive by American standards. Importantly you can both get on the course most of the time and also have no difficulty getting a game.

But be careful. Olympic breeds good players. "We've got 261 members with single-digit handicaps," says Callan, "and 22 that are scratch or better." These figures show the golfing strength of the Club; the organisational abilities of the set-up were demonstrated by the financial statistics. The 87th U.S. Open was big business, both for the Olympic Club and the San Francisco area. The club had a budget of £5.6 million to run the Championship, and were hoping to make about £500 000 profit. "We decided early on," said Bob Murphy, the Championship Director, "that we would run a good golf tournament and then hope to make a profit – in that order."

They received £2.3 million income from the letting of large, corporate entertainment tents, with another £1.2 million coming from smaller ones. Tickets that would get you onto the course and into the club house for the duration were priced at £106, and were selling for nearly £200 on the black market, which was

Olympic's trees could be a menace to the player, but a boon to the spectator.

not as much as it would have cost you to get hold of a ticket for a concert by the Grateful Dead the same week.

It was estimated that visitors to the San Francisco area for the Open would spend in the region of £9.3 million, mere peanuts compared to American Football's Super Bowl in 1985 which brought in £64 million.

◆　A CHANCE FOR A "PLODDER"?

The practising was complete, the preparations were over and the time for predictions had arrived. Who would win the 87th U.S. Open Championship was what 1200 representatives of the world's press wanted to know, and who better to ask on the eve of the event than Jack Nicklaus?

"Well it won't be me," he said bluntly. "I'll be lucky to break 100." Nicklaus had just played a practice round with Tom Watson and Roger Maltbie and between them they had managed three birdies. "No," he went on, "this course favours a plodder, a patience-oriented player, someone who doesn't try to be a hero."

There were good reasons for Nicklaus's opinion. The rough on the Lake course of the Olympic Club was fully-fledged USGA rough, deep and thick and clinging. Bernhard Langer started the week with six wedges in his bag in order to try to find the best way out of it, and it was largely due to the two that were still there

at the end of the tournament that he finished joint fourth.

Then there were the greens. After Australian Wayne Grady had completed his third round he launched into a tirade that went something like this: "This blank, blank course. Two great blank, blank shots at 18 and I'm eight blank feet above the hole. Then I hit a blank great putt which hits the blank hole and the next blank thing I know I've got a blankety blank 15-footer coming back."

They were fast alright. Russ Cochrane had an 8 foot birdie putt at the short 13th which turned into a 22 foot par putt and then a 4 foot

Even Craig Stadler's strength was no guarantee in dealing with Olympic's rough.

bogey putt, which he missed. Eight feet away in one, down in five. "A good club player," said Peter Alliss, "might four putt half-a-dozen times in one round on these greens."

One of the few players to hole anything on the 18th was Severiano Ballesteros, in his final practice round. Ten feet above the hole, he rolled it in, to the astonishment of the crowds, but not Sandy Lyle or Jose-Maria Olazabal. Only they knew that the Spaniard had the greatest possible incentive – had he missed it he would have had to have bought all three of them lunch.

The course, then, was tailored as usual for an Open. Raymond Floyd knew that defending his title would be almost impossible. Since winning, he said, he had stopped to smell a few flowers along the way, and anyway he was not in favour of USGA-style courses. "I loathe them," he said. "Last year at Shinnecock Hills was the first time they hadn't got the course the way they wanted it, and that was because the course wouldn't let them."

Jim Murray, of the *Los Angeles Times*, agreed with Floyd's assessment. He thinks the way the courses are set up produces unconsidered champions. "If the U.S. Open was World War II," he said, "Albania would win."

Floyd, aged 44, was talked out of it, and so was Nicklaus, aged 48, which was just as well according to Dr Ronald Lawrence, Secretary to the American Academy of Sports Physicians. "No-one over the age of 40 should play serious golf," he said. "It's bad for your health. On a fitness scale of 1 to 10, mountain climbing is 10, running is 7 and golf is minus 2. So, lacking a physical outlet, the body converts adrenal stimuli into anxiety, predisposing players to cocktails at the 19th." Now he may, of course, have been kidding. If not, that amounts to one of the finest adverts for golf I've ever heard.

So who could win? Greg Norman was the bookies' favourite, but he was not his normal, confident self. He confessed that, although he had got over Bob Tway's incredible bunker shot to rob him of the 1986 U.S. PGA title very

Marshall power. The unmistakable uniform caused mixed feelings.

quickly, it had taken him six weeks or more to forget the Larry Mize chip that took away the 1987 Masters Championship. "Every time I took a club in my hand I would see Larry jumping in the air and running all over the 11th green at Augusta."

Payne Stewart, we knew, would be trying. He told us so. Talking about winning a championship, he said: "I have been mulling over whether I really want it. Do I want to deal with the demands on my time, do I need a few more dollars? Now I have finally decided to try to win a major, deal with what goes with it and then see if I like it."

Watson liked the course. "It's a good, old-fashioned, lay-out and I wish we would build more. You don't have to move 2000 tons of dirt to build a green to be called an architect."

Tangling with the rough did not prevent Ben Crenshaw shooting a brilliant 67 to lead after the first round.

One man we knew would not win. Ian Woosnam wouldn't because Ian Woosnam couldn't. He was the only player in the top 20 of the Sony World Rankings not playing, which was a travesty. Third in the Open at Turnberry last year, winner of three tournaments in 1987, in the world's top 10 as rated by Ballesteros, and the USGA chose not to invite him. Worse, they had the power to pick seven players on the strength of their worldwide reputation and could only find six. They were Jumbo Ozaki, Isao Aoki, Tommy Nakajima, Rodger Davis, Mark McNulty and Jose-Maria Olazabal.

The USGA do not recognise the Sony system and their President, Frank Hannigan, said that they did not like commercial influences affecting their judgements. For how long? "I don't know," said Hannigan, "but when we sell out, we will sell out big."

A field of 156 set out to do battle with the 6709 yards of the Olympic Club's senior course. Twelve par fours, eight over 415 yards long, it played more than its length. Level-par 70 was a good score, 72 not bad and 74, while it may put you out of contention for the Championship, certainly no disgrace. The concensus among the players was that par would win. Seve did an opening 68 and said that he would happily accept three more 70's and not go out again. It wouldn't have been good enough, of course, but only by one shot, and there was not, at that stage, a single professional who would have disagreed with Ballesteros.

The Spaniard was one of seven players to break par, the leader being Ben Crenshaw with a 67. "This is a hold-on-for-dear-life kind of course," he said afterwards, and the man with the magical putter did just that. He holed a 60-footer at the 11th, a 35-footer at the 13th and said: "Good Lord, you don't expect those on Open greens. But they're a nice sight."

Not too many people saw such sights. Johnny Miller holed a few and even chipped in at the 16th. "At that stage I was feeling bulletproof," said the man who was a junior member at Olympic many years ago. "But the golfing gods decided to show me." At the 17th he bunkered his second, came out well above the hole, and took the obligatory three putts for a six. He was happy to get round in 71.

Ballesteros missed seven out of the first eight fairways and was still level par, an amazing achievement. He then chipped in for a birdie at the 13th and was delighted with his 68. "Usually I take 74 or 75 in the first round of the U.S. Open," he said.

Sandy Lyle, three-over after eight, was one of the few men to birdie the 17th, hitting first a one-iron and then a five-iron onto the green. Watson was another to birdie the 17th, after having bunkered his second. "I was looking at going four-over-par, when I holed that trap shot and got back to two-over. That was a key point for me."

Scott Simpson had halves of 35 and 36 for his 71.

◆ A MIXED BAG

Tom Watson did a 65 and the Championship became vibrantly alive. He hadn't won anything since 1984; no championship titles since the 1983 Open at Royal Birkdale. And there had been rumours. "I've heard everything as to why I'm in a slump," said Watson. "I've heard that I'm an alcoholic, that I'm divorcing my wife, that I'm giving up golf and going farming. None of it is true and I wouldn't care about it except for the hurt it causes my family."

Watson played his golf to some old tunes on Friday. "That was one of my top ten all-time rounds," he said. "I felt that I knew what I was doing. I haven't felt that confident for a long time. The light switch went on."

He talked frankly about his championship drought. He confessed that hitting one or two bad shots early on had been enough to get his chin on his chest and he also admitted that he had needed the 'kick in the rear' administered by his caddie when he arrived at the Olympic Club. "For the past couple of years, it's been like climbing a sandhill. I have just kept sliding back."

Watson's revival, on his way to a second round 65.

One of the keys to Watson's round was a 50-foot putt on the 3rd green. "I hit it far too hard and I hit it on the wrong line. If it had missed it would have gone 15 feet past, but it went in because the wrong speed and the wrong line cancelled each other out." When things like that happen to good players they can take advantage of them, if not by dashing off the course and taking out a mortgage on a house, then at least by going for a few more putts. So Watson was not surprised when a 30-footer fell in at the 9th, nor a 25-footer at the 11th.

That was the sort of thing that used to happen when Watson was winning championships, and it used to happen because he was not afraid of the 4-footer coming back. But once you lose that little bit of aggression, you lose the ability to hole the long ones.

Watson led by one from the man who said before the event that he'd be lucky to break 100, Nicklaus. The great man had found a way to get round without embarrassing himself, but he was still not happy. He offered some elemental thoughts on the game, and on getting older. Like all of us he had always assumed that he would grow older and wiser. Instead he found he was getting older and wilder.

"It's the easy part of the game that I'm losing, the actual ball-hitting that's going. I'm doing a lot of good things around the greens where I might have expected to start losing my touch with age. But the rest? I just can't figure it out. Through the years, whenever I've played badly, there has been a pattern. I've been doing one thing wrong and I've been able to figure it out. But now it's one up, one down; one right, one left; one off the tee; one out of the neck. I don't know where to start putting it right.

"You guys," he said to the assembled press corps, "you know that game. I ought to be your hero the way I'm playing."

This was a man who was two-under-par for the U.S. Open Championship but, as ever, he was being honest. He almost certainly knew it couldn't last.

He was tied with Langer, another player who was having trouble with the long game. In addition to the six wedges that caddie Pete Coleman had to carry for the practice rounds, he also had three drivers in the bag, and the West German, never particularly proud of his accuracy off the tee, felt that he was probably relying too much on his short game. "I can't believe some of my recoveries," he said. "Either they're miracles or I'm fantastic."

Lyle, with a 74 and Ballesteros, with a 75, were both unhappy with their games and were both behind a certain Eddie Kirby, a 24-year-old from Lincoln, Rhode Island, who had a total of 142 strokes on the board and just $61 in his pocket to last him until Monday. He hadn't really expected to qualify for the last two days and had, in any case, only been able to make the trip because members of his father's club had passed the hat round and raised $600. "I've got to play well to eat," he said. But at least he had that chance. Paul Azinger, at the start of the Open at the top of the US Money List, failed to qualify, as did Johnny Miller, Andy North, Calvin Peete and a man whose agonising as to whether to try to win a major was temporarily in abeyance, Payne Stewart.

Roger Maltbie made it, with rounds of 73 and 73, to get in by one. "That's not very good," he said, "but at least I'm still here. I'm not really

Seve's despair, on his way to a second round 75.

The Olympic foothills. Lanny Wadkins faces the long climb back to the 9th tee after losing his ball in the trees.

superstitious but I've got a good luck charm with me this week given to me by a man I know who used to caddie for Walter Hagen. He caddied when Hagen beat Bobby Jones in a match in 1926 and he gave me the penny that Hagen used as a marker. It's just such a lovely, lovely thought, that I'll use it."

There were not too many lovely thoughts in the minds of Sam Randolph and his father, though, at the end of the second round. Sam, a former US Amateur Champion, was suspected of playing slowly early on in the round and officials began to time his group. He was adjudged to be the guilty party and he was penalised two shots at the 17th. His four there became six, his 69 a 71, and delight became despair. Despite that, though, at least Randolph junior retained some sporting sense. As he entered the scorer's tent his father urged him not to sign the card in case they had some redress against officialdom. Randolph signed. "It was legitimate," he said afterwards. "I just don't seem able to pull the trigger."

Scott Simpson, with rounds of 71 and 68 was now joint eighth.

Seve's drive to the severely sloping 17th fairway in the third round, coming back into the reckoning with a 68.

The leader-board after day three of the Open was as strong in depth as anything produced by any major championship in recent times. Watson headed it, and within three shots were the likes of Ballesteros, Crenshaw, Langer and Mize. There was no Norman, and no Nicklaus either, but still enough quality to satisfy the most pernickety connoisseur. Norman, in fact, had never really been in the Championship, the only one of the last six in which he had not had a big role to play, while Nicklaus, using tabloid language, ran into what he called a 'bogey barrage'. He'd been expecting it, of course, and it duly came.

He played with Bernhard Langer and by the 6th hole was clearly fed up with the length of time the West German was taking over his shots. After Langer had studied his second to this hole, picked a club, then re-studied the shot and picked another club, Nicklaus deliberately went through the same tiresome routine, as if to make the point. But the fact is that neither man has been quick over the years, and while the authorities seem to have stopped fining Langer lately, they never even started with Nicklaus. If they had had the courage to do that, then the warning letters that had been pinned up in the Olympic Club locker room, on every player's locker, might have been unnecessary.

The USGA told every competitor in those letters that, in their opinion, 4 hours 3 minutes was as long as it should take to get round the course. The early rounds of the first day were taking 4 hours 33 minutes and, for as long as the officials at these championships shy away from taking action against *all* the slow players, all the letters in the world won't help. In any case, most of those letters were left where they had been taped, on the door of the locker concerned, unread.

Watson was on 208, after a round of 71, and he had to birdie the last hole, with a putt of 15 feet, to get past Keith Clearwater who, with a round of 64, had tied the course record held by Rives McBee.

Clearwater, a first-year rookie, had done a 64 before. In fact he'd done two of them back to back in winning the rain-affected Colonial National Invitational with 36 holes on the last day. This one he did the easy way, with six birdies and no bogies. Clearwater is a handsome, articulate young man, who thinks clearly. He told the world's press all about the way he had achieved his score, all about himself and then, as if getting impatient, said: "You know, I haven't done anything yet. So many guys have had tremendous rounds and then shot 87 on the last day."

If Clearwater was verbally touching wood, trying to guard against malignant fate, it didn't work. He shot 79 in the final round and finished joint 31st.

Much the same sort of thing used to happen to Tom Watson. But then, in the mid-70's, he started winning majors and hadn't stopped for nigh on 10 years. How would he feel tomorrow? "I'll be nervous, obviously. It's one of the most important rounds of my life. I know it and you know it. But I know how to win. I've done it before. It's just that I haven't done it lately. There is more courage involved, certainly for an American, in playing the last round of the U.S. Open, than in any other tournament."

Watson, an intelligent man, hadn't lost his sense of humour, though. He was asked how he would like to play the last three holes of the last round. "On the 16th, a good drive, a good iron, a good wedge to 4 feet and knock it in for a birdie. At the 17th, a 300 yard draw into the fairway, a low six-iron to 10 feet and topple the putt into the cup. On the 18th, with a four shot lead, you take the driver, hit a sand wedge to 4 feet and then you just go up to the ball and backhand it a few times until it goes into the hole."

Ballesteros, with Watson, was still one of the favoured ones to win, particularly after having seven birdies in his third round 68. No-one imagined that he would, if he had that chance

Rookie Keith Clearwater's 64 in the third round equalled the course record.

The Olympic forest takes its toll. Mark Wiebe (above) and Seve Ballesteros (below) were in trouble, but Tommy Nakajima (right) never even saw his ball again despite the help of a climbing spectator.

Watson's birdie putt on the 18th gave him the third round lead.

in the final round, use up five bogies as well. He was asked if he could win a U.S. Open on the tight courses associated with the championships. His answer was tart. "Many people think they know a lot about this game. But I know myself, how good I play. I know I have chance to win."

Scott Simpson had a par round of 70 and, for the first time in the week, he came to the notice of a few people, making the local papers for the first time. As he was joint second with Clearwater, this newspaper attention was practically obligatory, but no-one could get much out of this essentially modest man. "I'm a little surprised that a par round has put me in contention. When I came here I was really just looking forward to making the cut. At the start of the round today I was missing greens all over the place and just trying not to embarrass myself. But the Open's not that important. God and my family are much more important to me."

 ### THE MODESTY OF A CHAMPION

His first words were: "I just feel overwhelmed. I didn't think I was good enough. There are some great names on that trophy and to think that one of them's going to be mine. . ."

It is necessary to be realistic about Scott Simpson's win. He is good, with a sound method and, like many others, he occasionally putts really well. In 1986 he was 41st on the US Money List, in 1985, 39th. Such players occasionally win major championships. It does not, overnight, turn them into great players.

Simpson, aged 31, has left it late to become a great player. He will need to win a couple more majors to do that and the prospect of that is, frankly, unlikely. Not that he didn't play well when he had to. He holed some good putts and he hit three or four excellent shots when the pressure was at its height. But it all began with the little bit of luck that you need to win anything.

Time on their hands. Sandy Lyle, former British Open champion, with former US Open champions Larry Nelson and Fuzzy Zoeller.

At the 11th Simpson found the greenside bunker. In recovering he caught the ball a little thin and it shot straight at the pin, still at head height when it got there. Then it wrapped itself into the cloth and, instead of going through the green, fell down, 3 feet away. A possible bogey was turned into a par at a vital stage.

There followed, at the 14th, a magnificent seven-iron to 4 feet and then a 30 foot putt at the next for another birdie. "You don't really expect to make those," said Simpson. "That really gave me a lift." No sooner had he holed it than Watson holed from a similar distance on the 14th and now, although the two men were level at two-under-par, it seemed that Watson had regained the impetus he had earlier lost. Now, surely, the experienced man would win.

The 16th is a monster, unreachable in two, and Simpson, after a poor drive, hit a two-iron 120 yards short. Then he hit an average sort of wedge to 15 feet before producing a magnificent putt into the hole.

Watson, after two shots to 100 yards away, was standing arms akimbo, watching and waiting, and probably knew that he would have to match that birdie. He hit a wedge that pulled up 12 feet from the hole. But then he missed the putt. Now he had to rely on Simpson making a mistake, which he promptly did, hitting a four-iron into a bunker at the 17th. He had to stand above the ball, on the backslope of the bunker, and play to a green sloping away from him – and Ferrari-fast. It was an all but impossi-

Watson birdies the 14th to level with Simpson at 2 under.

Simpson's brilliant bunker shot at the 17th saved par and effectively won him the Championship.

Frustration for Bernhard Langer on the lightning fast greens, but he was in contention all four days, with a joint 4th finish.

Jim Thorpe playing his way into 9th place.

ble shot and Simpson, with a swing he will never better in his life, hit it to 6 feet. It was, furthermore, 6 feet below the hole and when that putt went in, the Championship was effectively won and lost.

Watson, who needed to birdie the last, took the wrong club for his second and said later: "I felt the breeze behind me as I prepared, and in my face after I'd hit the shot." The 18th, tree-surrounded and in a great natural ampitheatre, has that effect on golfers and all of Watson's experience could not shield him from it.

In fact Watson had lost the Championship early rather than late. He missed a short putt for his par at the 1st, went through the green at the 2nd and took three putts from 25 feet at the

5th: three shots dropped but, more importantly, a lessening of the pressure screws. The field was able to breathe.

Nevertheless Watson felt that he had got his game back. "The afterburners have been turned on," he said. "There's a lot of golf left in Tom Watson. But," he admitted, "I have to win to prove I'm back."

At least he got most of the way there, which is more than can be said for Ballesteros who, although he finished third, was not in it over the final holes.

He had started at one-over-par, three behind Watson, birdied the 1st hole and immediately looked a likely challenger. But he bunkered his tee shot at the short 3rd and,

Only four strokes off the lead after three rounds, Dale Douglass, 1986 US Seniors Open Champion, slipped to a last round 76. Gary Hallberg's distinctive hat (right) did nothing to help as he carded an 85 on the final day, having also been only four shots off the lead after three rounds.

although he played his expected brilliant recovery shot, he missed from 2½ feet for the par. He dropped shots at each of the next two holes as well, and, like Watson, had taken the pressure off the field. Then, when he had got his score back to level par after 11 holes, he drove into the trees at the 12th and three-putted the 14th, leaving the first putt 6 feet short. By the time he got to the 17th he was so demoralised and downcast that he left his first putt from 20 feet all of 10 feet short. "Sure," said a passing American journalist: "He wins all those French Opens, but when did he win a major last?" Answer: The Open Championship, St Andrews, July 1984.

On the face of it, Langer was also in the hunt, but in fact he never pressurised anybody on the last day. The nearest he got to Simpson was at the 14th, which he birdied to get within two shots. But he had no sooner done that than Simpson birdied the 14th, 15th and 16th to race away.

And so we come back to where we started from. The writers, perhaps cruelly, reminded Simpson, as he sat in the press tent savouring his triumph, that Nicklaus had said before the Championship began, that a 'plodder' would win.

"Yeah, that's me," said Simpson with a quiet smile. "I go for the middle of the greens, I make a lot of pars. I play my best on hard courses. Jack was right."

The final scene as
Tom Watson
prepares for his long
birdie attempt on the
72nd hole which he
needed to force a
play-off.

◆ SCOTT SIMPSON – THE INSIDER VIEW

Of course the most important part of any golf tournament is the post mortem. But with the U.S. Open there was something of a problem. Not many people had followed the winner's progress, and not many people knew much about the man. And with the new champion acting so modestly, it was hard to discover the background to the success story of the day. Eventually Simpson's caddy, Dan Stojak, provided some information. Stojak had spent 7½ years with Simpson and pointed out that this was not the first time they had been up on the leader-board at the death. He remembered: "In the Open at Pebble Beach he was in the last group and he was in the last group at Merion. I'd say he's finished in the top 15 in majors about 85 per cent of the time."

Simpson's wife Cheryl, a smiling, dark-haired Hawaiian American of Japanese extraction who has been married to him for ten years, was not inclined to write him off either. "I thought there was a good possibility he could win," she admitted. "He was playing really good and he was really calm. I just knew he would go out and do the best he could.

"He was working a lot on being calm and not getting angry at himself and I think that helped."

That was endorsed by Stojak: "He birdied the 1st, had a tough putt to save par at the 2nd and made that, then bogeyed the 3rd and 4th holes. You would think, if he was going to show any high temper or anything, that would have been the time. But he was very patient. Patience was the key word for the week and he kept it all the way through.

"That's just about what you're looking for, is pars," said Stojak. "It's not a golf course that yields that many birdies. On Sundays, usually, you can't really go for the pin on many holes. They're tucked away and you can't really get too aggressive because you could put yourself in a real bad situation. Just hit the green and two putt. He's the type of player that you'll see

do well on very tough golf courses," Stojak went on. "And any kind of major championship and you'll see his name up there. When they're shooting 25-under-par you won't see his name that often because he's still on the green making his par, making his up and downs, staying around par or a little under, playing the exact same type of game. But when guys are shooting just a couple under to win a tournament, that's where he's going to be. That's his game. He is an unbelievable up and downer," enthused the caddie. "Around the greens his sand shots and chips are just incredible. I thought this was lucky when I first started working for him but it happens week after week. There was one streak of about six months when he was holing about three chips or sand shots a week.

"We practise those shots a lot and do a little more at the majors, just concentrating on chipping, putting and sand shots around the greens. At Olympic we were practising an extra half-hour a day."

All the hard work and attention to detail paid off at the 17th in the final round when Simpson had an awkward lie in a bunker, with the ball below his feet. He splashed out to 10 feet and sank the putt to save his par and stay three-under, one ahead of Watson.

Stojak described his boss's sand shot as 'unbelievable'. "That was the turning point," he added.

Simpson himself looked serenely cool and calm all the way round. It was his wife and caddie who were feeling the pressure. Cheryl, who walked all 18 holes, admitted: "I got real nervous when he started making the birdies, I had to do a lot of deep breathing. I just had to keep on walking, stopping to watch him play, and taking a lot of deep breaths."

Even Stojak, who is an old hand at the bag-toting business, felt the occasion getting to him. "After 12 years, week after week, it gets a little hard to get pumped up any more," he said. "Everything is so routine. It's only when you're in contention that you get excited.

The moment of a lifetime for 31 year-old Scott Simpson.

"Scott had been in contention this year but I still can't remember the last time I was so nervous and I *was* feeling nervous out there Sunday. I was really feeling it, with the crowd and everything. At least my legs didn't give out on me going up the 17th," he laughed. "They were starting to feel like rubber a little bit but I had to keep going.

"It was really just super. Bruce Edwards, who works for Tom Watson, and I are real good friends and I kept looking back at him on the fairway as if to say, like, 'this is great'."

And so it was. The man to whom ABC television had paid no attention at all on the Saturday, when he was one shot behind Tom Watson, was walking up the fairway and into the record books. ●

Nothing make-believe about this putt. This one was for the Open.

THE OPEN CHAMPIONSHIP

MUIRFIELD, SCOTLAND

16-19 JULY

Nick Faldo's Open Championship began, two weeks before he teed off for his first round, with a 'phone call to Florida. He spoke to Dave Leadbetter, professional at Grenelefe, the man who has re-modelled Faldo's swing. After a few minutes of conversation, Leadbetter had agreed to fly to Scotland, to meet Faldo at Gleneagles and apply the final fine-tuning to the Englishman's game.

The two met up at the Bells Scottish Open, in which Faldo was playing. The tournament was a rich, prestigious event which, in the end, was totally dominated by one of the men who had swept past Faldo in the British rankings, Ian Woosnam. At one stage in the final round the little Welshman led by 11 shots; he finally won by seven, with Faldo miles behind in 21st place.

To everyone but Faldo and Leadbetter it was yet another disappointing finish. This pair, in fact, had given the tournament only fleeting attention. They had actually spent four days together, working on the practice ground, refining the changes to Faldo's swing. They were only small adjustments to a game that had already worked well enough to win the Spanish Open – on a course set up to his own specifications by Seve Ballesteros – in May.

Faldo had also finished second in the Belgian Open, but these were really only minor milestones on a road that was headed for far greater things. Faldo wanted to win the Open Championship. He always had done and, like anyone who has ever actually holed a putt to win an Open, he told us afterwards of the thousands of make-believe putts he had holed, and missed, which were 'this for the Open'.

He wanted to win, in fact he knew he had to win, if he was to regain his status as one of Europe's leading golfers. In 1983 he had been European number one. He had won five tournaments, three of them successively, and, as the winner the following year of the Sea Pines Heritage Classic, there seemed no good reason why he should not continue to dominate the European scene. He was not regarded as the equal of Seve Ballesteros, but then, at that time, no-one in the world was, and to be second only to him was genuine star status.

But everything in this apparently rosy garden was far from being lovely. The week before the Sea Pines event Faldo had contended strongly, for three rounds, in the US Masters at Augusta. But come the final round he collapsed and there were a few harsh words telephoned back to England by the British press. There were a few cutting headlines, too, but the one that infuriated Faldo in fact never appeared. He was told, wrongly, by a caddie, that a London tabloid had labelled him 'El Foldo' when, in fact, the tag, if it ever existed, did so only in someone's embittered imagination.

But Faldo, at first, was not to know that. He was as furious as anyone would be at such a vicious appellation and he played the Sea Pines tournament in a state of controlled fury. Only once did it overspill and that was when I made the trip down to see and report Faldo's imminent triumph. I arrived on Saturday to find Faldo still leading after the third round and when he turned up in the Press room to be interviewed, I went forward, as the sole British pressman present, to congratulate him. He glared at me, said "What were your headlines last week, then?" and turned away. I had no idea what he was talking about, for I had not heard about the 'El Foldo' allegations, and was not to find out until the next day.

Faldo duly won the tournament. By interview time he had cooled down and I told him that no-one, to my knowledge, had used such a headline and a tentative relationship was re-established. But 'El Foldo' did not go away. There was just enough hurtful basis for it in his failures to win that Masters and also the 1983 Open at Royal Birkdale, for it to stick in the minds of the golfing caravanserai that follows the world's tours. And eventually, if not because of the tag but because of the failures themselves, Faldo decided that he would have to do something about his swing.

To almost everyone in the game, Faldo's swing was a thing of beauty. It should have been a joy to him forever. But rightly or wrongly Faldo became convinced that there was, somewhere, a technical flaw that would prevent him from realising his ambitions. He maintained that it was not sufficiently solid to play 18 holes under the kind of severe pressure that comes into play on the last day of a major championship. Nothing would do but to dismantle it, and to reconstruct something

that would. The man he turned to was Dave Leadbetter.

Florida is full of golfing gurus. Every other club has one and the trick is to find someone whose methods suit you and, most importantly, in whom you can believe implicitly. Leadbetter was such a man, although at first Faldo thought he could pick his man's brains and incorporate only certain facets of Leadbetter's Law into his swing. He was quickly disabused of that idea. Leadbetter not only told him that it had to be all or nothing, he also said that it would take two years to incorporate all the changes so that they became second nature. There was a stage, for instance, when Faldo was using a Leadbetter backswing but a Faldo downswing and it was hardly surprising that confusion reigned on the course and chaos crept into his bank account.

In Europe, in 1984, he went from 1st to 12th and, in 1985, to 42nd. In America he was 38th in 1984, 117th in 1985 and, last year, 135th. By the time he reached Muirfield he had lost his player's card in America – but he also had a secret weapon. The changes to the swing were complete.

They were, in extreme brevity, a flattening of the swing to eliminate a tendency for the right elbow to fly and a change of clubhead angle at the top of the backswing. Armed with the confidence that everything was working well, with the reassurance offered by Leadbetter at Gleneagles, Faldo felt that he could face anything that the fairest links in golf could throw at him.

But in addition to the swing changes, Faldo was, personally, a changed man. Over the years he has had a distinctly prickly relationship with the men whose job it is to report his deeds. He was always ready to co-operate after a good round, less so when he had played badly and when we wanted to know why. He was wary of the press, perhaps with good reason after he had been pursued by certain sections of it during the break-up of his first marriage, to Melanie. The gossip columnists

Nick, Gill and Natalie Faldo with the Open trophy.

rang up at all hours of the day and night, pestered him in restaurants and hotels and even, on one occasion, staked out the place in which he and his wife-to-be, Gill, were eating. He escaped them by fleeing through the kitchens, and memories of that kind do not dissolve lightly.

It was not only the gossip writers. The golf writers were not entirely trusted either, after some acrimonious clashes over the years. There was the business with Sandy Lyle during a tournament in Africa when Lyle, to prevent the fierce sun reflecting into his eyes from the head of his putter, stuck some elastoplast on it. Faldo said nothing at the time, but at the end of the round reported his partner for changing the playing characteristics of the club. His complaint was upheld, Faldo finished ahead of Lyle, but the golfing world in general would have been happier if he had said something to Lyle on the course.

Then there was the infamous Graham Marsh incident in the Suntory World Match Play Championship. During the playing of the 16th hole Faldo hit a shot that would have gone into an almost impossible position through the back of the green had it not been intercepted, and thrown back onto the green, by a spectator. Neither player, nor any of the officials, saw this, but it showed up clearly on television and the next day Faldo was berated for taking advantage of it. The papers, in general, claimed that he should have either conceded the hole to Marsh or, at the very least, given him the three foot putt that Marsh missed to take three putts and lose a hole he should have won.

That was a harsh judgement, for there was just enough confusion at the time to present a defence for the way Faldo conducted the affair. But what was less defensible was the way he behaved the day after. Asked if he regretted the way things had gone, Faldo spurned a great chance to make his name as a sportsman. He could have said, simply, that he would not have wanted to win the way he

A misty Muirfield witnesses Faldo's final putt.

did and that having seen the television replays, apologised to Marsh. Instead he said nothing of the sort. He said that he had been forced to do what he did. This was the World Match Play Championship, he said, not the Wentworth Christmas Alliance.

That was a response as unfortunate as some of the criticisms of his original action, and for a few years the press-player relationship, which is so vital to golf, was soured. But all attitudes change with time, and earlier this year, the man who took the pictures for this book, Phil Sheldon, had dinner with the Faldos. Without of course knowing the great things that were to follow, he sensed a softening of Faldo's attitude to the press in general. He had become a father, to Natalie, and had begun to sense that there might be, after all, life beyond the fairway.

In a press conference after he had won the Championship, Faldo talked about his ambitions, and said that he had realised that while winning an Open meant everything to him, there were people to whom it would mean nothing at all. "After all," he said "if you don't play golf, that," and he indicated the old claret jug of a trophy that stood in front of him "means nothing."

It was an altogether more mature attitude, one that did him credit, and he told us, too, of some of his plans for the future. A small part of his time was going to be spent rearranging the decorations at home. "I've only got one picture hanging on the wall at the moment," he said. "It's a signed one of Tom Morris Senior." Old Tom had won the Open some 126 years before Faldo and it was obvious that a picture of the latest in a long and very illustrious line of champions was going to join the great man of another time.

◆ AT THE HOME OF SEAMUS MACDUFF

The press tent before an Open Championship is a practical place, full of pragmatists. Its occupants seek to make reasonable prose out of

professional pronouncements like: "I hit the ball good, hit a buncha fairways and holed a buncha putts." A man who can prove he has been doing all that on a reasonably regular basis is usually installed as favourite for the forthcoming event.

But what is to be made of someone who says: "I went to the Sonora Museum in Tucson recently and there was a plant there which only grows in two places in the world, in Arizona and the Sahara. And it's identical and it wasn't transplanted." That doesn't come into the category of 'a buncha' anything, nor did a later comment. "I love coming to Scotland. It's where the Kingdom is. It's where Seamus lived."

Tom Watson, formerly a student of psychology at Stanford University, was the man talking and his comments need, and deserve, some explaining. The first was a perfectly reasonable attempt to explain why American golf was no longer dominant in the world. More people play, in better conditions than ever before, for more money and under greater pressure: it is obvious that some of them will flourish.

The second comment was more abstruse. The 'Kingdom' referred to by Watson is the Kingdom of Fife, just across the Firth of Forth from Muirfield. Seamus is Seamus MacDuff, a character in a book by Michael Murphy called *Golf in the Kingdom*. The book is regarded, variously, as the ravings of a lunatic, a gigantic leg-pull or, by one American critic as 'either a book about golf seen through mysticism or a book about mysticism seen through golf.'

What it is to the average golf punter is rubbish and an object for scorn and derision. But Watson, certainly not your average punter and a man versed in pyschological ways, has clearly read and enjoyed these strange outpourings of the man who founded the Esalen Institute in California and has edited the *Journal of Transpersonal Psychology*.

But it surely takes a quite exceptional mind to draw help or comfort from the kind of

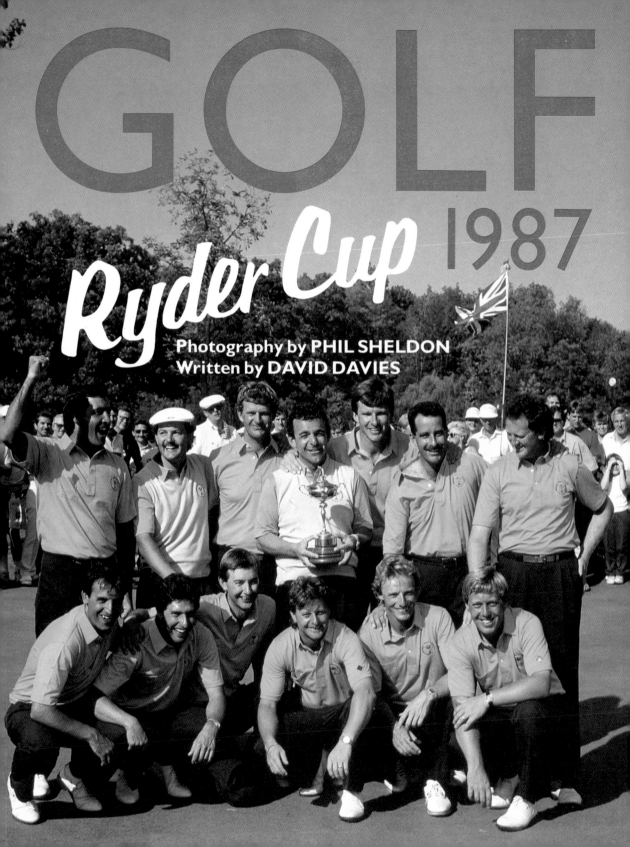

GOLF

Ryder Cup 1987

Photography by **PHIL SHELDON**
Written by **DAVID DAVIES**

Stalking the prey. Seve Ballesteros and Jose-Maria Olazabal.

THE RYDER CUP

MUIRFIELD VILLAGE, COLUMBUS, OHIO
25-27 SEPTEMBER

Everywhere, on every day, in every series, there was great golf being played. The essence of the Ryder Cup is, of course, that it is a team effort, but within that framework there is room for individual feats which, at Muirfield Village 1987, occasionally stretched the credulity.

◆ THE LEADING PLAYERS

Every player contributed positively to the team, but no-one, of course, more so than Seve Ballesteros. The Spaniard has accepted his regal role in European golf and he has, to his credit, also accepted the responsibilities that go with it. He attracted huge crowds for all his matches, and for the first two days he shepherded Jose-Maria Olazabal through his Ryder Cup debut. He did it to such effect that, when he played comparatively indifferently on the afternoon of the second day, Olazabal was able to take on the task of winning the match as if he had five Ryder Cups behind him.

Ballesteros might have been created especially for match play, such is his pride in performance and his delight in destroying the opposition, either on or off the course. He plays all his golf with an intensity that is often frightening to witness.

But, perhaps most importantly for Europe, Ballesteros established a moral stranglehold very early in the proceedings. On his first hole, a par four, Ballesteros was short of the green, Olazabal about 4 feet away in three. Seve wanted his partner to putt out so that he could then have a 'free' chip but Strange immediately objected, saying that the young Spaniard would be standing on the line of his putt and could leave spike marks. It seemed a slightly dubious objection to the people present, but Ballesteros just said, "Okay, no problem" and simply chipped the ball into the hole, from 40 feet, for a birdie.

Tony Jacklin called Seve 'Superman', saying that when he got into these situations he became a changed man. Even Nicklaus joined in. "I don't have a Seve on my team. At the present time I think Seve and Greg Norman are head and shoulders over the rest of the world."

But if Ballesteros led by the sheer force of his personality, then others touched his hem and found similar inspiration. Statistically, the four best players in the match were all Europeans: Ballesteros, Woosnam, Faldo and Langer, the latter three getting three-and-a-half points to Seve's four, while Lyle and Olazabal equalled the best of the Americans, Tom Kite and Hal Sutton, by getting three points each.

It is no coincidence that those six Europeans were paired with each other. Langer asked for Lyle, Ballesteros agreed to Olazabal and Woosnam and Faldo were made for each other.

Woosnam is 5 feet 4½ inches of barely controlled aggression. In a matchplay situation, into which a little patriotism is mixed, you know one thing about Woosnam: he will fight to the utmost of his ability and, even if he fails, the other fellow will know he's been in a scrap.

It is a kind of boxer's aggression that Woosnam takes with him onto a golf course, and it is the fact that he has natural handspeed that enables him to hit the ball such immense distances. He lost his singles to Andy Bean, but nevertheless made a huge impression on him. Bean is a foot taller than Woosnam and at 16 stones 7 lbs, is five stones heavier. He looks the part of a long hitter and, by almost every golfing standard, he is. But Woosnam outdrove Bean on every hole on the front nine and on all but one of the back nine, to the obvious astonishment of the American. "Shoot, he's strong," said Bean afterwards. "It hurts when a little bitty fellow out-drives you."

Woosnam's partnership with the largely unflustered Nick Faldo worked wonderfully well. The Englishman's urbanity matched the Welshman's passion and it produced the goods.

Faldo needed the lashing length of Little Woosie; Woosnam needed the precision of Faldo to convert it into points. Faldo now has the best record of any European in the Ryder Cup. At the start of proceedings he had, remarkably, won more Ryder Cup matches than Ballesteros and Lyle put together and, while that no longer applies, he took his record to Played 22, Won 14, Lost 6, Halved 1. That is a magnificent effort and one which indicates that, despite his apparent reserve, there is a great team player within him.

In recent years Faldo has re-modelled his

Nick Faldo and Ian Woosnam. The long and the short of it, but an ideal partnership.

swing and the man who did the job, David Leadbetter, was at the Cup. At the start of the week there was some fine tuning done, a few slight adjustments made. And under pressure conditions at Muirfield Village, the swing, and Faldo, were fine. There were times, too, when the reserve slipped. Faldo had both feet off the ground, both arms in the air, when Langer hit his fabulous shot in the Saturday afternoon fourball matches, exulting, as he should, at another vital point gained.

Langer, at first sight, is another player you would not expect to be a team man, or a man capable of allowing his emotions to show. But the apparently impassive, allegedly relentless West German is far more affable than he appears. He does more talking on the course than almost all of his contemporaries and it was this willingness to communicate

Sandy Lyle's prodigious length and Bernhard Langer's steadiness, a formidable combination.

that lay at the root of his row a few years ago with Ballesteros. Seve goes into a cocoon of concentration on the course and does not talk to anyone but his caddie, and then only to berate him. Langer is not like that at all and nor, of course, is Lyle, and that is probably as good a reason as any other why they made such a good partnership.

There was a moment, at the 5th hole on Saturday, when Langer drove into a ditch and looked out of it. But he didn't have to worry, because Lyle, with a huge drive and an even bigger four-iron, was on the green of this par five, 531 yards, in two, just 15 feet from the hole. It was a possible eagle, a certain birdie, and with both the Americans in trouble, the hole was as good as won. A few minutes later the two men walked off the green all smiles.

Langer knows about, because he has been

afflicted by, the game's fallibilities. In his early career he had the yips, was almost incapable of holing out from 3 feet or under and three putt greens, with the occasional four putt, were common. But he has gritted his way out of it. He has won a major championship, the US Masters, on probably the fastest and most severely sloped greens in the world and to do that you have to be not just a good putter but, for a week at least, a great one.

It was Langer, of course, who did not putt the putt that won the Cup. It was, in American parlance, called a 'good-good'. This means that if the two balls are roughly the same distance from the hole, and each player agrees that the others need not be putted, then each player's putt is 'good', hence 'good-good'.

Langer approached his singles opponent, Larry Nelson, on the final green with Nelson's ball about 2 feet from the hole, Langer's less than that. The German looked at the American and Nelson, after a brief pause, picked up both balls. In that moment, Europe won the Cup. Ballesteros was behind, dormie two and certain of at least a half-point. It is almost certain that Nelson did not know the exact position but it nevertheless made a fitting end to what had been an extremely sporting occasion.

Lyle is most people's idea of the absolutely ideal fourball partner. The only limits to his talent are those he sets, often unconsciously, for himself. He believes in percentages, he plays cautiously more often than not, and he still wins and makes huge amounts of money. But when he casts those constraints aside, he becomes a different man.

Lyle also knows that if his partner is someone as good as Langer then a par at the hole is a virtual certainty and so he allows himself some freedom. The result at Muirfield Village was some monstrous hitting: hitting so huge that it reduced Jack Nicklaus to baffled resignation. Nicklaus designed the par fives at Muirfield Village so that one of them, the 11th, would almost always be unreachable in two and two of the other three would be out of range no matter which way the wind was blowing. Of Lyle, and his hitting, he said: "He plays all my par fives with a drive and three-iron and all my par fours with a one-iron. You're not supposed to be able to do that, in fact it's not allowed."

The last of the leading scorers was a slightly shy young man with a lovely sunny smile, Jose-Maria Olazabal. He got all his points in partnership with Ballesteros, but that is not to belittle his contribution to the proceedings.

He is a considerable golfer in his own right and to have achieved all that he has done – second in the 1986 Order of Merit, two European tournaments won and now a Ryder Cup place – by the age of 21, is incredible. Jacklin asked Ballesteros if he would play with Olazabal as much because of the compatibility of their games as for any other reason. There is no better exponent of the short game than Olazabal, not even the man he was playing with, and it was graphically illustrated on the 18th green in the Saturday foursomes. Ollie, as he inevitably is known, drove well but Ballesteros bunkered the second shot. It was a fiendishly difficult explosion but he got the ball to 8 feet.

Because the Americans were making a mess of the hole, the Spaniards now had to get down in two to win the match – and Ballesteros putted almost as far past the hole as they had been when they started. Olazabal

Spanish joy for Ballesteros and Olazabal as the latter holed the winning putt on the 18th in their foursome against Crenshaw and Stewart.

The sun rises on the 1987 Ryder Cup as Torrance and Clark versus Strange and Kite make an early start.

then holed the return putt and it was total relief that made Seve charge across the green and clasp Jose-Maria to him in a bear hug. The young man did an awful lot of growing up on that green.

◆ THE GREAT MATCHES

Friday morning foursomes

Lanny Wadkins and Larry Mize versus Ian Woosnam and Nick Faldo

Everything was going wrong. After all the inspirational words, the comfort taken from the fact of 1985 and the intellectual appreciation which said that we had a better team than they did, the position after nine holes of the opening series, the Friday foursomes, was that Europe was three down in the top match, three down in the second match, four down in the third and two down in the fourth. There was obviously a very distinct chance that we would lose the opening series 4-0 and if that had happened then the Ryder Cup would almost certainly not have been retained.

Not only would it be physically difficult to come back from such a position, the mental aspects would be crushing. It would have been a reversion to all those years when the American side only had to show up to cause the quaking in the boots and a near-automatic loss.

Europe desperately needed some inspiration from somewhere and it was to come from two men – the 1987 Open Champion, Nick Faldo and the leader of the Epson Order of Merit, Ian Woosnam. Faldo had been strangely muted during practice, consulting with his guru, David Leadbetter, at every practice ground session, apparently still not satisfied with the swing that had taken him to that famous victory in July. But it was to be him, nevertheless, that began the European recovery, striking a magnificent three-iron second at the 10th which finished only 3 feet away. Four down became three down and the mood changed. Wadkins became unsure of himself, hit into a bunker at the short 12th and into a stream at the 14th and suddenly the Europeans were only one down.

At the 15th Faldo hit a good drive while Mize, who has to draw his tee shots to get any length, clattered into the trees on the right, leaving Wadkins with a 330 yard second if he wanted to get on the green in two. But it was Woosnam who found the length. He smashed a one-iron 250 yards, off an uphill lie, into the breeze and over a deep dell in front of the green, pin high, 15 feet away. Not only was it a hole-winning stroke, it was a game-winning stroke and, in retrospect, a Ryder Cup winning stroke in that all that followed might not have been possible without it.

As Woosnam's shot landed on the green, to a huge roar from the small European supporting contingent, Mize and Wadkins exchanged glances. It was only a brief moment, and no words were spoken, but it was significant. For the first time there was obviously doubt in the minds of the Americans, doubt about that particular match and, probably, doubt about the whole outcome.

The British pair two putted for their winning birdie and from being four down, six holes ago, they were now level.

It was Mize to drive at the 17th and, remembering his mistake at the 15th, he overdid the correction process and cut his ball miles right. It was the worst possible place to be, behind a stand of trees and leaving Wadkins with a 200 yard shot, out of rough, demanding 40 yards of fade. He was not up to it, leaving the ball short and right of the green, in even thicker rough. Mize's recovery attempt went under the ball, which flopped into a bunker and amazingly incredibly, the Europeans were now ahead. It needed only a safe and solid par four at the last, which Faldo and Woosnam duly supplied, for a notable victory. It was the end of a beginning for the Americans, as well as being the beginning of the end.

Jack Nicklaus, American non-playing captain can only manage a wry smile for his cheerleaders ..... He smiled even less later as Crenshaw and Stewart lost their foursome against Ballesteros and Olazabal.

Larry Nelson had never been beaten in any Ryder Cup matches. In 1987 his final tally was lost 3, halved 1.

Jack Nicklaus, ever gracious on and off the c

About 2000 European supporters lined the course .....

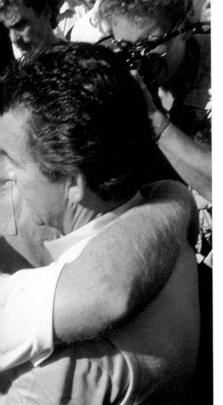

.... celebrations at Lyle and Langer's brilliant win on Saturday ....

e, congratulates Tony Jacklin.

.... and a lot more celebrations after the presentation on Sunday.

Saturday afternoon fourballs

Tom Kite and Curtis Strange versus Nick Faldo and Ian Woosnam

Going into the afternoon fourballs Europe held a 8½-3½ lead and there was an air of optimism, not to say confidence, in the camp. They would have settled for what actually transpired, a 2-2 result, but they could not have known how it would be arrived at. It was, quite possibly, the finest sustained exhibition of golf ever played. It was a case of be brilliant, or lose. Strange and Kite were five under par when they lost while Nelson and Wadkins holed Muirfield Village, all 7104 yards of it, in an eight under par 64, and lost on the last green. It was barely believable drama.

Kite and Strange were undoubtedly America's top pair. They were unbeaten and, as number one and six in their country's Money List, were heavily relied upon. After five holes of the fourballs on this day, they were five down. Faldo and Woosnam began with five birdies between them and although the Americans birdied two of the next three holes, they made no progress for so did the Europeans. If ever golf could truly be said to scintillate, then this was it. Faldo and Woosnam had gone out in 29, seven under par, on a course that is generally acknowledged to be one of the most difficult in the world.

They were five up, and were to go six up at the 10th with yet another birdie. There was a bemused look on Strange's face as he walked to the 11th tee, but still no lack of determination. He and Kite birdied the hole, plus the 12th, to get back to four down, but holes were running out.

Faldo and Woosnam were 10 under par after the 14th and, with the most birdieable of the par-fives still to come, then 11 under was almost a certainty. Even allowing for no more birdies, then a score of 61 at Muirfield Village still does not seem possible, and it is likely that these two players will never again play so well collectively.

Faldo and Woosnam were 6 up at this stage of their spectacular fourball versus Strange and Kite which they went on to win 5 and 4.

Larry Nelson and Lanny Wadkins versus Sandy Lyle and Bernhard Langer

Lyle and Langer were only nine under when they won! But whereas Kite and Strange never had a real chance of victory in their match, Wadkins and Nelson were in with a chance right down to the last green. There has been plenty of drama in the Ryder Cup, but it is difficult to conceive that there has ever been anything better than this match.

The Europeans were, generally, in charge, and when Lyle hit first of all a monstrous drive at the 15th, and followed it with a three-iron onto the green and followed *that* with an eagle putt of 15 feet they were three up with three to play.

But as so often happens, when a side gets into a desperate situation, then they play their best golf. Wadkins, particularly, revels in such things, and he hit a tee shot at the short 16th to 5 feet. Two down and two. Then, with the pin in an impossible position at the 17th, leaving a landing area of about 10 feet, Wadkins, because he had to, went for it – and made it. He also made the putt. One down and one.

All four players hit good drives to the last hole and Nelson played first, getting safely onto the green, leaving Wadkins with the 'free' attacking shot. But first it was Lyle to play, and, in a gathering gloom and with a posse of PGA officials, players, wives and pressmen watching, hit his eight-iron to 3 feet.

The match seemed to be just about sewn up. Lyle could, of course, miss but Nelson was unlikely to hole from where he was, and Wadkins had still to play. Then the American pitched his ball 12 inches from the cup. As it flew unerringly at the pin there was a huge crescendo of noise from the crowd who, for a moment anyway, thought it might go in on the fly. But it did not, and, worse, it rolled onwards up the green to about 10 feet. Holeable, certainly, but still Lyle would have to miss his.

Now it was Langer's turn to play. After Lyle had hit his shot he turned to the German and said: "Get inside that and we'll be alright," and

Team spirit. Lyle helps Langer up after holing his chip on the 10th hole.

Langer was, of course, in a position to try.

He hit an even better shot than had Wadkins. Like that of the American it also flew at the flag, but this shot pitched just short, took a hop forward and came to rest inches from the hole. Even in the circumstances of needing every possible point and having to investigate every possibility, there was nothing the Americans could do about this shot. It had to be a 'gimme', and, to their credit, they picked the ball up unhesitatingly. It was a fantastic end to a fantastic match.

Of the match Tony Jacklin said: "I never thought I would live to see the day when I would see golf played like that." Nicklaus was of a similar opinion: "They played beautifully. They beat our rear ends," was his assessment.

Sunday singles

Larry Mize versus Sam Torrance
Ben Crenshaw versus Eamonn Darcy

To retain the Ryder Cup – three-and-a-half-points. To win it outright again, just four from 12 singles matches. In theory it was simple; in practice almost unbearably difficult. The Americans had the edge almost throughout the day as they fought for what Nicklaus had conceded would be an incredible recovery. He knew it was all but impossible, but he also knew that with defeat on their home territory looking oh so likely, his team would fight harder than they knew how.

In a day of incredible pressure the first to crack was Dan Pohl. His defeat at the 18th, to Howard Clark was to be followed by an amazing match between Sam Torrance and Larry Mize.

Also on the 18th, Sam Torrance had an interminable wait in the middle of the fairway as Larry Mize, who was one up, sorted out his drive which had finished unplayable on the bank of a stream on the left. He had to take a penalty drop, could not reach the green with his third and now it was Torrance to play after about 15 minutes of hanging around. He seemed to be going about his job a little too quickly, but he had the shot he wanted to play sorted out in his mind and he crashed a seven-iron onto the green. Mize hit a poor chip but then, to roars of encouragement, holed a 20 foot downhill putt. Now Sam had to get down in two for a half-point, and, with that superbly slow putting stroke of his, slid the ball dead from 10 feet.

But the day's highest drama was to follow. Eamonn Darcy had been picked for three

Sam Torrance halved his match with Larry Mize at the 18th.

Ben Crenshaw putts with a one-iron after breaking his putter in anger.

Ryder Cup teams before this one, and had never gained a single point. Then he lost his only other match in this team and, after having been three-up on Ben Crenshaw – who was putting with a one-iron having snapped his putter in anger – was now all-square on the 18th tee. The omens were not good.

But again it was the American who cracked. Crenshaw found the same stream as had Mize, took a drop and hit his third into the front greenside bunker. Again it was the European who had the nerve-jangling wait and Darcy, going for the pin, fell just short with his second, into the same bunker as Crenshaw.

The American came out to 5 feet below the hole, Darcy to 4 feet above it. It was almost the hardest putt on the green and it became a great deal harder when Crenshaw holed his for a five.

Darcy took an age over surveying his putt, but then he stood over it, hit the ball almost straight away and in it went. There was immediate uproar. Darcy was one of the most popular members of the team and his colleagues had felt for him and his lack of points. Now he had not only a point, but a vital one at that. It was, for him, the moment of a lifetime.

The popular Eamonn Darcy holes out at the 18th for a crucial win against Crenshaw.

Langer and Nelson concede putts on the 18th for a halved match and Europe retains the Ryder Cup.

Seve Ballesteros beats Curtis Strange on the 17th to consolidate the team victory.

Larry Nelson versus Bernhard Langer

Bernhard Langer had been three down to Larry Nelson after 11 holes and seemingly out of it. Three holes later he was all-square and back in the hunt. There were five matches on the course now, and from somewhere a full point was needed. Langer was level, Ballesteros and Brand were leading, but the latter's lead was rapidly being eroded by Hal Sutton. It was tight, tight, tight and Langer, it was felt, had to come through with at least a half. They reached the 18th all square, they both hit the green, albeit Nelson only just, and a few moments later they were both within 2 feet of the hole.

Langer was the closer and, as he walked towards his ball, he looked enquiringly at Nelson. It took the American some time to work out that what Langer was suggesting was a conceded half and then, with an instinctive gesture, Nelson bent down and picked up both balls. He almost certainly did not know it, but with that half-point that he conceded to Langer, Nelson also conceded the Ryder Cup. It meant that the sides were tied at 14 points each and as that also meant that America could

not win, Europe retained the Ryder Cup.

It was an historic moment. Never before in America, never twice in a row. It was also a deeply satisfying moment. To go to the home of Jack Nicklaus, to a course designed and built by him, to beat a team captained by him, was something to be savoured indeed.

Back on the 17th, Ballesteros and Strange had reached the green and the Spaniard holed from under 2 feet to beat the American number one. That, together with Gordon Brand Junior's eventual half with Sutton, meant a margin of 15-13 and the celebrations were immediate. The European supporters took over a huge barn-like bar at the back of the 18th green and there they sprayed each other with champagne, supplied by the match sponsors, Johnnie Walker whisky.

The 18th green, said Derek Lawrenson of the *Birmingham Post*, was awash with the colours of Europe, and so it was. Twenty thousand star spangled banners, handed out to the spectators as they came through the gate in a vain effort to boost the American bid, had to be furled as Europe, gloriously, won the Ryder Cup ●

Friday, 25th September

		EUROPE		U.S.A.
MORNING FOURSOMES	S. Torrance and H. Clark	0	C. Strange and T. Kite (4 and 2)	1
	K. Brown and B. Langer	0	H. Sutton and D. Pohl (2 and 1)	1
	N. Faldo and I. Woosnam (2 holes)	1	L. Wadkins and L. Mize	0
	S. Ballesteros and J. Olazabal (1 hole)	1	L. Nelson and P. Stewart	0
		2		2
AFTERNOON FOURBALLS	G. Brand and J. Rivero (3 and 2)	1	B. Crenshaw and S. Simpson	0
	S. Lyle and B. Langer (1 hole)	1	A. Bean and M. Calcavecchia	0
	I.Woosnam and N. Faldo (2 and 1)	1	H. Sutton and D. Pohl	0
	S. Ballesteros and J. Olazabal (2 and 1)	1	C. Strange and T. Kite	0
		6		2

Saturday, 26th September

MORNING FOURSOMES	J. Rivero and G. Brand	0	C. Strange and T. Kite (3 and 1)	1
	N. Faldo and I. Woosnam	½	H. Sutton and L. Mize	½
	S. Ballesteros and J. Olazabal (1 hole)	1	B. Crenshaw and P. Stewart	0
	S. Lyle and B. Langer (2 and 1)	1	L. Wadkins and L. Nelson	0
		8½		3½
AFTERNOON FOURBALLS	I. Woosnam and N. Faldo (5 and 4)	1	T. Kite and C. Strange	0
	E. Darcy and G. Brand	0	P. Stewart and A. Bean (3 and 2)	1
	S. Ballesteros and J. Olazabal	0	H. Sutton and L. Mize (2 and 1)	1
	S. Lyle and B. Langer (1 hole)	1	L. Wadkins and L. Nelson	0
		10½		5½

Sunday, 27th September

SINGLES	I. Woosnam	0	A. Bean (1 hole)	1
	H. Clark (1 hole)	1	D. Pohl	0
	S. Torrance	½	L. Mize	½
	N. Faldo	0	M. Calcavecchia (1 hole)	1
	J. Olazabal	0	P. Stewart (1 hole)	1
	J. Rivero	0	S. Simpson (2 and 1)	1
	S. Lyle	0	T. Kite (3 and 2)	1
	E. Darcy (1 hole)	1	B. Crenshaw	0
	B. Langer	½	L. Nelson	½
	S. Ballesteros (2 and 1)	1	C. Strange	0
	K. Brown	0	L. Wadkins (3 and 2)	1
	G. Brand	½	H. Sutton	½

FINAL RESULT	EUROPE 15	U.S.A. 13

Front cover. The winning European team: Seve Ballesteros, Gordon Brand Jnr., Sandy Lyle, Tony Jacklin (non-playing captain), Nick Faldo, Sam Torrance, Eamonn Darcy. Front row: Jose Rivero, Jose-Maria Olazabal, Ken Brown, Ian Woosnam, Bernhard Langer and Howard Clark.

Published by Partridge Press, Maxwelton House, Boltro Road, Haywards Heath, West Sussex
Supplement to *Golf: The Major Championships 1987*
Printed in Great Britain by W. S. Cowell Ltd, Ipswich   ISBN 1-85225-047-X

PARTRIDGE
PRESS

passages that figure in the book. The other principal in the book, alleged to have been a real, true-life figure, is called Shivas Irons, a professional with whom Murphy played a round and who employed some strange methods, like these: 'He stooped down gracefully to tee his ball, balancing for a moment on one leg, as if to test his balance and spring. It was a kind of ritual dance he was to repeat on several holes. Then he stood addressing the ball for a few seconds... like Ben Hogan he seemed to peer into the very centre of the ball and summon a secret strength. I could feel the energy gathering, feel it in my solar plexus, a powerful magnetic field drawing everything into itself.'

And that was only on the first tee. Wait until we get to the 13th: 'Shivas went into the oddest ritual of all. First he stood on his left leg, then on his right, once with eyes open, once with them closed. Then he cupped his hands to his mouth and gave an incredible cry. It was a long wavering wail, something between a yodel and a cry for the departed dead. It sent a shiver up my back.'

Most people who did that would get sent a swift letter from the committee, enclosing their subscription back, but Shivas (who got round in 67, incidentally) was apparently only trying to communicate with Seamus MacDuff. Murphy, not unreasonably, asked who MacDuff was.

It turned out that the 13th was haunted. 'Seamus MacDuff,' said Shivas Irons, 'is the man who invented the game so long ago. He's working on it still, perfecting it you might say.'

Now all this is alright at leg-pull level. But golfers in extremis, golfers who have lost the knack, golfers who have tried everything that technique and technology can offer, turn occa-

Tom Watson, the thinking man's golfer.

The favourites who never made the leader board: Severiano Ballesteros and Greg Norman both found trouble in the same bunker at the 18th on the first day. Ian Woosnam, fresh from winning the Scottish Open by seven shots, could not find the same form at Muirfield.

sionally to matters of the mind. But I hope Tom Watson does not really believe all this stuff. Blood curdling shrieks are all very well in their place, but not, please, at an Open Championship.

◆ THE SAD SPANIARD

Severiano Ballesteros, at the Muirfield Open, was a sad man. He scowled a lot. At 30, of course, the youthful exhuberance is on the wane for most people. Ballesteros, who is not most people, was experiencing those symptoms even more fiercely. The first intimations of golfing mortality had arrived.

At Muirfield he was bitter about the fact that he had not won a major championship, to go with his two Opens and two US Masters titles, since the 1984 Open at St Andrews. He did not like the fact that others, patently less talented, had won, while he had only come close. He said: "I am waiting for my week. Others have had theirs and it is time for me to have another." The implication was that the luck had deserted him, always the refuge of a losing golfer.

But it was not just on the golf course that there was dissatisfaction in his life. Left to him he would have been a married man for some time. But his fiancee's father, President of the Bank of Santander, is old money. Ballesteros, son of a fisherman, is new and the class system in Spain is rigid.

Then there was the matter of playing golf itself. Earlier this year Mitchell Platts of *The Times* found himself sitting next to Ballesteros on an aeroplane, and produced a remarkable interview, run by his paper on the eve of the Championship. It said, in part: 'When you meet and marry a woman you have a special love for her and that love continues. But as the years go by, and I am sure people will understand, there is a different kind of meaning to that love. It is no different in golf. I still get the same excitement from the competition but you cannot expect, as the years roll on, to have

the same feelings. We grow older, we mature. I remember Tom Weiskopf saying to me several years ago that once upon a time he went to sleep and couldn't wait for the morning to come so that he could play golf again. I know exactly what he means. But that is moving further away. Somewhere out there on the course I lost my youth. I never realised how much the winning and the money would change my life. It is the pressure. I expect too much of myself. I seek absolute perfection, but I am a human being, not a machine.'

Poor little rich boy, perhaps, but the pressures *are* enormous and they *do* increase as the years go by.

◆ THE PRESS AND THE PRIZE

Nick, of course, 'nicked it'. Most of the popular papers said so. And he was, naturally, 'Fabulous Faldo'. In fact, some of the headlines combined both puns as they screamed out the news of the win. 'Fabulous Faldo Nicks Title' said the *Daily Mail,* while the *Star* said 'Nicked It – Faldo Hangs On To Clinch A Humzinger'. The *Mirror* resurrected 'Land Of Open Glory' with 'Ice Cool Nick Swings It' underneath, while two other papers took the fact of 18 par figures in the final round as their cue. 'Par-Fect Faldo' said the *Express,* while the *Scottish Daily Record* said 'He's Par For The Course'.

All good punny, if not particularly funny, stuff. But at least there was no doubt that he was a worthy champion and the headlines and the articles underneath them proclaimed that fact. Paul Azinger may have finished bogey, bogey, but it was Faldo who had put him under pressure, and there was no begrudging the Englishman his glory. Except possibly, by the Muirfield club itself.

Shortly after Faldo had won, there emanated from the area of the 18th green the extraordinary sound of booing. There has never before been such a noise at an Open and it turned out to be nothing to do with Faldo, or any of the players, but directed at the organising officials of the presentation ceremony.

They carefully placed the tables and chairs in such a position at the back of the 18th green that while the privileged members of the Honorable Company of Edinburgh Golfers could see everything, very large numbers of the general public, including many in the huge stands, could not see a thing. They were, naturally, upset at not being able to see a British champion·collect his trophy and it is a considerable reflection on the character of the game, and of those who play and support it, that the booing was only mild. In other countries there would have been a riot.

Afterwards one member of the organising committee tried to blame the photographers for obscuring the public's view, a piece of arrant nonsense and an unfortunate illustration of how little some of them really care for the people whose game it is. David Miller of *The Times* quite properly thundered: "There was nothing particularly honourable about the Royal & Ancient prize-giving ceremony. . . The presentation to the winner and runner-up should be properly public and not partially hidden from the view of many. . . The moment should be grand, not primly genteel. The glory belongs to the winner, the runner-up and to the people who have followed their duel."

What else did the papers say? There was, of course, a lot of instant speculation about how much money Faldo might make out of winning the title. He employs Mark McCormack's company, the International Management Group, to look after his affairs, and they are the same people who have made around £2 million for Sandy Lyle out of his win. The speculation, then, began at about £3 million for Faldo although there has to come a time when the law of diminishing returns starts to operate. Faldo is the fourth European in recent years to win a major championship, behind Ballesteros, Langer and Lyle. Any tournament that wants any of those four to play will now have to pay. Ballesteros costs the earth – anything up to £50,000 depending on whether he wants

to play or not – and Langer costs about half that. A promoter wanting all four might have to pay out well over £100,000 in appearance money before the thing even gets off the ground.

With prize money also increasing, the cost of staging a tournament is spiralling and there must come a moment, presumably, when sponsors call a halt. Faldo will probably make his money, but the next championship winner will have to be a charismatic character if he is to continue to make the millions that such a title is supposed to generate.

The other player in the piece was, of course, Paul Azinger. Totally unknown on this side of the Atlantic (except, perhaps, for the more retentive of *Guardian* readers, for whom I had reported his win in the Phoenix Open earlier in the year) he was the leader of the American Money List by a mile when he clocked in for the Open.

He had won over half-a-million dollars in six months, and the expenditure of $10,000 on a Concorde flight for himself and his wife barely made a dent in that. At first meeting he seemed to be a personable young man, a member of the US Tours Bible Study Group, along with Larry Mize and Scott Simpson, the previous two winners of major championships in 1987.

Tall and lean, and with a strong grip, he did not, though, seem to be best fitted for links golf. As late as the day before the Open you could have got a good price on Azinger from any of the bookies, with William Hill, for instance, offering prices on 15 players at up to 33-1, without mentioning Azinger. The theory was that, although he was having such a wonderful season in America, having won three tournaments, he had not been around long enough to win a major. After all, his best finish in one had been 17th, in the 1987 Masters, and he would surely not be able to cope with the demands of links golf, especially with its attendant winds.

But that did not stop a few people having

a dabble, mostly each way, on this new name and it is a fact that of some 350 bets placed from within the press tent during the week, there were about a dozen on Azinger and only one on Faldo.

Perhaps if people had scrutinised Azinger a little more closely, there would have been even more action. He learned his golf in Florida, a state where they know all about wind, and his progress through the various levels of the game once started, has been remarkably consistent. He took three goes to get his Tour card but, having done so in 1984, promptly won $80,000 in 1985. Last year he increased that to $250,000 and, of course, he had hit the jackpot earlier in the 1987 season.

When I saw him in Phoenix he was in the process of winning his first tournament on Tom Weiskopf's course in Scottsdale. This is one of the Stadium courses that are so popular these days in America and has been created, quite literally, out of desert. Weiskopf shifted millions of cubic feet of sand and dirt and finished up with a course that I found very attractive. There is, strangely enough, more than a hint of links about it; albeit the weather in Arizona bears very little resemblance to anything ever experienced by the side of the Firth of Forth.

Azinger won his tournament well. The last hole at Scottsdale is a demanding par-four and Azinger needed one to win. He got it comfortably. In the press room afterwards he gave the distinct impression that, although he was delighted by winning, he did not regard it as being in any way a one-off. Not that he is in

Larry Mize (left) and Scott Simpson (above), the winners of the previous two major championships. Both fell victims of the weather on the third day, with scores of 76 and 82 respectively.

Amateur Freddy George is first to tee off in the Open Championship at 7.30am.

any way boastful. In fact, the reverse. He was asked what, if anything, he was doing with his sudden accumulation of wealth and said that all he had bought was a stereo cassette player for a pick-up truck he drives around. Was that when the Ferrari was in for repairs? "If I got out of something like that in front of my high school friends I'd be embarrassed."

◆ DOWN TO BUSINESS

Tom Watson called Muirfield without a wind a 'naked lady', presenting no challenge. Had the field known what was about to occur in the 116th Open Championship they would have fought for her favours on the first morning, as it dawned warm and windless. It was the last time that the weather was to be even approximately normal and those who went out in it were lucky indeed.

The principal beneficiary of the good weather was Rodger Davis, he of the plus-two's

Rodger Davis's new course record of 64 on the first day gave him a seven shot lead.

and the diamond socks with 'Rodger' embroidered down one leg and 'Davis' on the other. He went round in 64, setting a new course record for Muirfield. Isao Aoki did his 63 in the 1980 Open before the course was lengthened. Davis called it one of his best-ever rounds and anyone who starts an Open with a round of seven under par is obviously going to be very pleased with life. Davis was, and the round played a large part in his eventual second-place finish. It was not that long before this score that Davis was very unhappy with life. He was fed up with golf, having acquired the twitch, and decided to devote all his savings to opening a motel on the Queensland coast. Two years later, and £200,000 to the bad, Davis was bankrupt and he had to return to golf. But by now the twitch had gone away and so had his habit of finishing second so many times. He won the Whyte and Mackay PGA Championship in May of last year and since then has won over half-a-million dollars on circuits around the world. An ebullient Aussie, he deserves his success.

Davis was playing with the man regarded as the best British hope for the Championship in the pre-tournament speculations, Ian Woosnam. But he could not get into the round, and although his 71 looked satisfactory at the end of the day – because the weather forced up later scores – it was not a good performance. He was not to be a threat on this occasion.

But Davis's other partner lasted longer. Craig Stadler had 67 blows in a round that was officially recorded as a 69; this was because of an extraordinary two-stroke penalty.

Stadler drove into the rough at the 5th where he found his ball embedded in the ground. Now Stadler has played most of his adult life on the US PGA Tour and so he knew what he had to do in this situation. He took a free drop, played the ball out and got a birdie four. Except that he didn't. There were several spectators dotted about at the point of the incident and they were mystified when Stadler was shown to have birdied the hole.

They may not have known about the rules of the US Tour, but they knew the Rules of Golf, which state quite clearly that in such situations you have to take a one stroke penalty. Stadler was duly reported and when he got to the scorer's tent at the end of his round, was asked what has been going on. Stadler, in innocence, told them and was then assessed his two-stroke penalty. With commendable calm he came into the press tent and told us about the incident and agreed, when pressed, that he was 'not real pleased' with the way things had gone.

Stadler is, of course, the man who lost $38,000 earlier this year through his ignorance of the rules. He laid a towel on the ground to protect his trousers from the mud when trying to play a kneeling shot from under the branches of a tree. That was held to be improving his stance illegally and it probably cost him a place in the Ryder Cup team too.

Both Faldo and Azinger had 68s with the latter feeling that a good ball-striking round was about to get away with no tangible reward when suddenly a few putts fell and left him a satisfactory three-under. Faldo experienced an incident even more bizarre than Stadler's. Half-way round the course the scoreboards started putting up a message for his wife, Gill, to return to the clubhouse. It could have distracted him if he had started to worry about it, but he carried on, coccooned in concentration.

It turned out to be nothing serious at all. Nick's wife, Gill, likes to walk the course with her husband, but since the birth of Natalie 10 months ago, gets little chance. But on this day Ian Wooldridge, the *Daily Mail* columnist, offered to do a little baby sitting, and off went Gill.

Faldo birdied the first three holes – he was to say later that unless you do that you certainly can't birdie all 18 – and during that time Natalie was, in the words of Norman Mair, of *The Scotsman,* 'as good as gold'. But she burst into tears when: "Dad could manage no more

After the incident at the 5th on the first day, Craig Stadler was not so keen on the rough.

than a routine par at the short fourth. Of course," continued Mair, "it may only have been coincidence. . . but Wooldridge, though at least plus-6 as a sportswriter is apparently a 24-handicap nanny." Natalie had cried so hard, it seems, that she broke out into a rash, which only disappeared with the re-emergence of Mum.

The wives of professional golfers have to be an independent breed, well able to amuse themselves, take decisions and cope with all those family problems that crop up when the man of the house is the man on the course. Or the practice ground or, often, thousands of miles away.

They have their own pressures, then, and it helps when a body like the Royal & Ancient do their bit to help relieve them. At Muirfield Angela Bonallack, wife of the R&A secretary, Michael, arranged a coach trip to Edinburgh. The Royal Mile was traversed, the Georgian House in Charlotte Square visited and a couple of hours were devoted to shopping in the Grassmarket. "I tried to keep them away from the cashmeres," joked Angela, "so they would buy them all at the Open." Among those present: Linda Watson, Tom's wife, Chrissie Kite and Claudia Trevino.

"We realise," added Angela, "that the wives probably don't want anything too organised but we like to give them the option of a trip and we want them to feel welcome."

◆   ROUND TWO

This was the day when, quite apart from adding a 69 to his 68 and going joint second in the Championship, Faldo displayed to the world a mature and responsible attitude to the winning of big events. "When you're playing in these championships, or on a difficult course in anything, it is not the great shots that you play which are the truly important ones. It's much more a question of where the

Faldo takes a free drop on the 17th, but 40 yards back from where the ball had finished, and still the rough to contend with.

bad ones go. If you hit it off line then the best thing is to take your medicine and get it back onto the fairway. The thing to do becomes to get away with the least possible score. You must not take risks if you're in the kind of rough there is here."

The rough was long, but it was made worse by the incessant rain. It became clinging, twisting the clubface so that you could never be sure of where a shot would go even if struck well, and there were disasters galore. Faldo almost had one at the long 17th, which was playing short on the day and yielding many birdies. Faldo's drive was cut and vanished in the general direction of the Exhibition Tent. It was found, but had to be taken to an official dropping zone which happened to be 40 yards back from where Faldo had finished. It was also a fairly unpleasant place to have to drop a ball and Faldo could only hack an eight-iron forward down the fairway.

That left him, on this potential birdie hole,

with 150 yards to go to the green and he had to hit a seven-iron for his third. It was not a particularly good shot, finishing 30 feet from the hole, but when Faldo holed it, it was one of those significant moments, at least in hindsight. To birdie that hole after playing it the way he had was a very real bonus, the kind that wins championships.

There was one other key moment in the round. The drenching rain had, by the 9th, got through to everything and Faldo decided on a dash to the locker room to get a dry towel. "The grips to my clubs were saturated," he said. "If I couldn't have got another towel things would have been very difficult." In such seemingly insignificant ways are titles decided.

There is, as Raymond Jacobs of the *Glasgow Herald* reminded his readers, always a duty intruder at the top of the leader board in an Open. This year it was Gerard Taylor, an Australian whose biggest claim to fame was that he had once won the Papua New Guinea

Teamwork.
Australian Gerry
Taylor and
matching caddie.

Jack Nicklaus the caddie. An unusual sight as Jack caddies for his son in the prequalifying.

Open. That, and the manner of his qualifying for this championship.

Taylor had been at North Berwick when, standing on the tee of the 18th, a short par-four, he was told by a friend that he needed a two to get into the play-off. He promptly drove the green and holed from 30 feet for the eagle. North Berwick was the course where Jack Nicklaus Jnr. had tried to qualify, causing one of the Championship's great sensations when his father decided to caddie for him. Jack Senior had been having dinner in the Marine Hotel when he looked out of the window at Junior playing a practice round. He went out, walked a few holes, offered to caddie and was accepted.

On Sunday and Monday there were several hundred people at the course, simply to watch the great man push a cart round for his son, and it was, in a way, unfair for Junior's playing partners, who had to cope with unexpected pressures while trying to get into the Open. Nor was Senior much good at the job. "If I was caddying for me, I'd sack myself," he said afterwards, adding that his competence was matched by the fee he was being paid – "nothing."

Azinger was to lead by one at the end of the day, having hit, at the 18th, one of his best bunker shots ever. He got it to within six inches despite it lying on a downslope and having no room with which to work. "I used to be just awful at trap shots," he said afterwards. "But last year I led the stats in that category and I did it by sheer hard work. I would go into a bunker and stand there for an hour hitting shots."

It was a handy ability to have at Muirfield, where 150 bunkers dot the course, some of them evil little glue-pots that are reluctant to release your ball at all. Arnold Palmer, in fact, got into one that he could not get out of. It happened at the 14th, a par four, and he took 10. It also took him out of the Championship, 'buried', as Tim Glover suggested in *The Independent* 'by the sands of time'.

"I feel as if I was in there for days," said Palmer afterwards. "I was right up against the bank and the ball was half-buried. I had taken a bogey at the 13th, I was angry and I wanted to take it out on the next hole. But I guess it took it out on me. I was digging a hole for myself in there, but I wasn't going to come out sideways, there were too many people watching for that." He took five goes to get it out, getting onto the green in eight and two putting for double figures.

Afterwards, talking ruefully to a bunch of reporters, he came out with a remark that will live in the history of disasters. "I wouldn't say that God couldn't have got the ball out of that trap, but He sure would have had to have thrown it."

A week later, at the Senior's British Championship, one member of the press tried to get him to talk a little more about it. "I remember it," he said with a touch of asperity, "but I am not interested in being reminded about it."

◆ THE EXHIBITION CENTRE

'The greatest golfing show on earth' is a fair description of the Open Championship. Even most Americans will concede that, and one of the things done on a scale far bigger than anything found at the other major championships is the Exhibition Centre – a vast tent housing close to 100 exhibitors ranging from club manufacturers and knitwear specialists to booksellers and jewellers. During Open week over 100,000 people are likely to wander round, browsing and buying.

Walter Elliott, who has worked for Pringle, the knitwear firm, for nearly 50 years, was attending his 31st consecutive Open and remembers the first Exhibition, which was a rather more modest affair at Hoylake in 1956. *"Golf Illustrated* pitched a tent and invited suppliers in. There must have been almost 18 to 20 of us and it was all very rough and ready. We could park our cars round the ropes, we

The tented village at Muirfield provided an important business venue, as well as shelter for spectators. . .

ate in the clubhouse and the toilet facilities were a bit primitive – a dry bucket outside the tent.

"We were the only knitwear people; now I reckon there are over 40 stands selling knitwear. Everything was more homely then. There weren't so many overseas players – it was the time of Peter Thomson and Bobby Locke and I do remember Hoylake was Gary Player's first Open. Everything has grown up gradually and it's now a lot bigger – and cleaner."

Walter did his early selling out of cardboard boxes. Now all the stands are fully equipped with shelving and 40-foot articulated lorries bring in the merchandise. At Muirfield, the Royal & Ancient, who took over the running of the Exhibition at Sandwich in 1985, even supplied a buggy service to and from the lorry park to help exhibitors stock up rather than have them staggering across the fairways with armloads of jumpers, golf balls or whatever.

At a conservative estimate Pringle expected to sell £100,000-worth of goods during their six-and-a-half days of trading at Muirfield, with the wives of the American and Japanese players being their best customers, buying up sweaters for themselves, their husbands, friends and family. Over the years Walter has become friendly with people like Winnie Palmer, Barbara Nicklaus and Viv Player. He was too discreet to say whether they were the Big Three of shopping.

They obviously appreciate the service. Barbara Nicklaus has been known to go and get the coffee for hard-pressed sales staff and during the Bill Rogers Open at Sandwich, Walter was the recipient of some Oriental hospitality. "I took three Japanese wives up to our showrooms in London," he explained, "and I thought I'd just have a sandwich or something light for lunch. But they insisted on taking me

. . . however, many braved the terrible conditions on the course. Tom Watson strides amongst the umbrellas.

out for a proper lunch and then I joined them for a shopping expedition."

It would have cost Pringle in the region of six to seven thousand pounds for their stands at Muirfield – even before paying for their manning and so on. The smallest unit available cost about £800. One of the people responsible for constructing the whole thing is John Ratcliffe of J A Tonge Ltd, exhibition organisers, consultants and contractors to the R&A. The firm has been involved with the Open for as long as Walter has. The tent at Muirfield measured a massive 425 feet by 100 feet, that still being 75 feet short of the biggest one ever, which was at Birkdale, where there is more room.

In John's terms the best venue is the one with the flattest floor, and that accolade goes to Birkdale. "We were on a concrete tennis court," John remembers, "and that means we had no worries about subsidence. At Muirfield

this year, for instance, we started sinking because the grass, which had been particularly long, was thoroughly trampled by the combined weight of thousands upon thousands of people. We had the carpet and the floor up every night to put in extra packing to build it up. We use sacks of plywood and off-cuts under the flooring. We also had problems at Troon where we were on the ladies' course. One of the bunkers had been filled in and the sand settled and part of the place started to sink."

Rain can be a major problem, not least when it drives people into the tent and remains so heavy that they do not leave. "There was a potential panic at Sandwich last time in 1985," says John, "when there was torrential rain and too many people in the tent. No matter how many tannoy announcements we made they wouldn't move and the whole place was bunged. Fortunately there was no major accident and we have contingency plans should it happen again."

The Exhibition Tent, situated on Augusta Avenue, just along from Penina Path (David Hill, the championship secretary and George Wilson, the deputy secretary of the R&A are the men responsible for dreaming up the names of the main thoroughfares in the tented village and the hospitality complex, where you could stroll along Turnberry Thoroughfare, round Carnoustie Crescent and up Birkdale Boulevard) went up on June 18, nearly a month before the Open started on July 16. Construction of the stands started on June 22 and was finished on July 10, three days before the first customers arrived on the first practice day.

Breakdown took one week and only a large yellow patch showed where thousands upon thousands had tramped, trying on, taking off, swishing clubs, putting with something that might just provide the answer to those three-footers, having the Muirfield logo embroidered on sweaters, caps, towels, buying umbrellas and booking holidays in places where golfers don't need waterproofs, just sun block. All the nails and bits of metal used in the construction were swept up by a special machine using magnetised discs, developed by John Ratcliffe because the tent had been previously sited on a rugby pitch at St Andrews and the debris was an extra hazard scrummagers and tacklers did not need. It is not only in golf where the Open leads the way!

◆   THE THIRD DAY

This was the day that competed for a place in the history books. Heavy, prolonged rain with fresh-to-strong winds was the prediction, and, as is the way with forecasts for bad weather, it was correct. Unbelievably over 25,000 people turned out to watch what they could see of the golf, which causes question marks to be raised about the levels of sanity in the East Lothian region. It was a simply loathsome day and although it was just about playable, in the strict sense of that word, it was the kind of day that makes you wonder just how golf ever managed to catch on. Peter Dobereiner, of the *Observer*, suggested that it proved conclusively that the game could not have originated in Scotland: no-one would ever play something that demanded spending three or more hours abroad in that kind of weather.

It drew comparisons with other foul-weather days of the Open, including the one at Prestwick in 1881 when only eight players completed the Championship, won by Bob Ferguson of Musselburgh. The R&A Championship records describe the day, and its events, thus: 'The small number who completed the Championship is largely explained by the weather. It was the day of the Great Storm, in the course of which 180 fishermen were lost round the coasts of Scotland. The peaks of Arran were covered in snow.'

Over a century later sleet was reported in Dundee, and no-one had much stomach for golf. Sandy Lyle had to go out in the worst of it, and in what was, technically, the round of the championship, scored a level par 71. The *Mail on Sunday* called him 'The Iron Lion', which deserved to catch on. He used a one-iron to keep the ball low and, at the time that he did it, it seemed that it might take him a significant way up the leader-board. But comparisons to other record bad days were weakened by an easing of the elements later on, and the leaders played in weather that was merely awful.

Greg Norman was upset that he had had to cope with the worst of it for most of the round, and he came in to tell us that he thought two-tee starting was a good idea. It would, he said, mean that fewer people would get the extremes of the weather, but he failed to explain how it could be operated at a course like, say, Lytham where it would be a 15 minute journey by road to get to the 10th, or at Troon where the 10th is about two miles away down a rough track. He also failed to explain, satisfactorily,

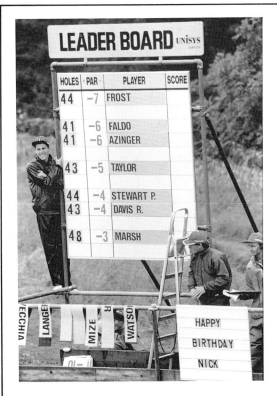

HOLES	·PAR·	PLAYER	SCORE
44	−7	FROST	
41	−6	FALDO	
41	−6	AZINGER	
43	−5	TAYLOR	
44	−4	STEWART P.	
43	−4	DAVIS R.	
48	−3	MARSH	

HAPPY BIRTHDAY NICK

Nick Faldo's 30th birthday on Saturday, and just one stroke off the lead.

why he wanted to legislate that kind of luck out of the game, although no-one had the temerity to ask him if he would like the sport played indoors, in, say, a hermetically sealed balloon to protect everyone from everything.

Faldo and Azinger played together on what was the former's birthday. He had not received a present from his wife because whatever it was that he was getting was too big to be brought to Muirfield. All Faldo knew was that it was made of wood and, in a flash of humour that contended for remark of the week, he surmised that in view of the weather it might be an ark. Nevertheless, he and the American had the best of it, and it had relented enough for them to be painfully slow. The R&A keep making noises about slow play and saying that

Trevino's dislike of the cold was only made stronger at Muirfield. . .

they really must do something, but they allow players in their championship to fall holes behind and then not take any action. Faldo's excuse was that he was not *playing* slowly, just taking a long time. The photographers were the main problem, he said, because they

South African David Frost was in contention until the last round, but finished in 6th place.

Head injuries? American Ken Green (above) and Australian Graham Marsh (right) had somewhat unusual headgear to combat the weather conditions.

Saturday afternoon. Faldo and Azinger played together and both found trouble at the 18th.

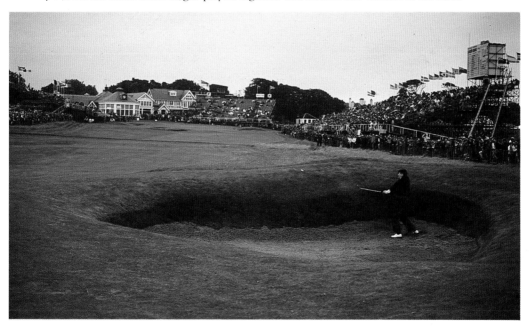

At the end of Saturday, Azinger had a one shot lead over Faldo.

had to get to their positions for each shot and it was far better to wait for them to do that, than get cross and blame them for a bad shot afterwards. That is certainly a mature consideration, but if it is the real problem, which I doubt, then it should be easily dealt with.

Faldo ended the day just one behind, dropping a shot at the last. He hit one of the shots of the day, a two-iron second into 'a howling left-to-right wind, with the pin on the left' which he thought was 'a helluva shot'. But it ran just off the green, his chip ran 8 feet away and he missed a putt he deserved to hole.

Azinger, who said that he had never even seen weather like he had this week, let alone played in it, was content with his position. For an apparently frail player he was handling the wind and the rain with considerable ability, although he confessed that he had had the best of the weather all three days. He, too, took five at the last, although it was a good, or a bad five, depending on your point of view. He drove into a bunker, the first time he had done so all week, took a sand wedge to get out and then missed the green with a four-iron third. Eventually he holed from 13 feet for a bogey. "I desperately wanted to make that putt and I was proud to do so and have the lead.

"No matter what happens tomorrow I am going to be a better player when it is over. You cannot get this experience anywhere else. This is the greatest place in the world to play golf and I am in the best position I could be and I am enjoying it. But I know I have a long way to go in golf. I know how bad I can hit at times. Winning here, well that would just be the icing on the cake of a year that has been pretty good to me so far."

◆ THE FINAL ROUND

The moment for Nick Faldo to win the Open Championship arrived nearly 200 yards from the 72nd green at Muirfield on Sunday. He both recognised it, and welcomed it. It was the moment he had been through purgatory for, changing and refurbishing his swing, and enduring a good deal of rubbishing from his critics.

Now he needed a par four at the hole that Jack Nicklaus has called the hardest finishing hole in Championship golf. It is 448 yards of bunker bestrewn terror· and Faldo had negotiated the tee shot safely. He was roughly 190 yards from the green, a distance that would normally call for a four-iron, but which, on this occasion, was to be played with a five. Faldo, under the most extreme pressure, was thinking with marvellous clarity and he knew that with the extra adrenalin coursing through his body, any club he hit would travel further.

"You can't imagine what it's like to try and play golf under those conditions," Faldo said afterwards. "It's like those heart-stopping moments when you think you're going to be involved in a car crash. You go all hot and cold.

"It's such an important moment, and yet it is over in seconds. I had to hit the shot and I didn't know if I could, but I knew it had to be done. Then, suddenly, I'd hit it and there it was flying straight at the green. All I could think was: 'Cor, look at that.'"

Faldo hit the five-iron of a lifetime. There was still work to be done, of course, but when, the next morning, Faldo awoke at 5.30am, it was that shot that was in his mind. "I couldn't believe it," said the new Open Champion, "I was still hitting that five-iron."

His new swing and, just as importantly, his new confidence, had been equal to the moment. The whole of the previous two years had been devoted to the task of making sure that if he ever got into a position to win a major championship, he would have the armoury to do it. On the afternoon of July 19, 1987 he proved he had.

At that moment, of course, he was actually one behind the only man who could take the Championship away from him. But Paul Azinger, in a moment of sheer stupidity, had taken his driver off the 17th tee and driven the ball into a pot bunker from which he could only come out sideways. Lee Trevino had done the same thing in 1972 and only by a fluke – chipping in from the bank at the back of the green – had he got a five and gone on to win. But Azinger did not have that kind of luck with him.

Up ahead Faldo still had a couple of crises to survive. He had to get down in two for his four, of course, and he had to do so after Craig Stadler had, unwittingly and unwontedly, tested his nerve still further. Stadler had hit a poor second into the crowd, by the railings, and had to send for an official so that he could take a drop. That took time, as did the playing of the shot, and then he had to putt first as well.

All Faldo could do was stand there, nervously lick his lips and unconsciously hitch his right arm jersey sleeve up with his left hand. It is an old and unvarying habit when Faldo is in tense situations, and there could hardly have been a tenser one than this. The sweater itself was yellow, with a pattern on the front that resembled the blueprint for some complicated electronic circuitry, and Faldo would no

The final hole. Azinger's bunker shot had to be close but wasn't. . .

. . . the 30 foot putt had to drop but didn't. . .

doubt have welcomed a robot to take the putt he was having so long to wait for.

When eventually he got round to it, he hit a truly awful first putt. "I thought to myself that as a kid I'd stood on greens saying 'This to win the Open' and when I looked at that 40 footer at the last I thought 'This to win the Open.'"

But the putt was far too ambitious. It raced 4 feet past the hole and the crowd groaned. It looked like the prelude to three putts and a bogey and a chance lost. But that was not how Faldo was looking at it. "I said to myself 'Don't dribble it, hit it firm,'" and he did, and it went in. The crowd were delirious. They all knew that Azinger, who had by now taken his six at the 17th, would have the devil's own job of getting a matching four and they cheered Faldo for several minutes. Faldo, himself, departed into a hut by the side of the green, signed his card and then resolutely refused to watch either of the two television sets that were showing the final stages.

Eventually Azinger hit his tee shot, a good one with the one-iron he should have used off the 17th tee, and he too had a five-iron second into the green. But Azinger was playing in his first Open, contending in his first major, and the pressures for him were unbearable. He hooked his shot, it flew with what must have been sickening certainty for the American, into the bunker on the left.

Now Azinger is the best bunker player in America according to the statistics, but the final cruelty was that the ball landed on the back-slope of the bunker, within an inch or two of where, earlier, Gary Player had been. "As soon as I saw where he was," said Player later, "I knew Nick was the Open Champion. I had been there and hit one of the best shots I could ever hope to hit and even getting a bit lucky into the bargain I was 15 feet away. I thought he would do well to get anywhere closer than 20 feet."

The American had to stand with one foot outside the bunker, the other in the sand and,

The presentation ceremony. Faldo is the second Briton to win in three years.

sure enough, he got nowhere close. The crowd applauded his failure, as they had cheered the shot that went into the bunker, and while it is a difficult situation, the spread of this kind of poor sportsmanship has to be stopped somehow. It had happened when Dave Graham bunkered his second at Royal St George's when Sandy Lyle won and it left a bad taste in the mouth then.

The Chairman of the Championship Committee, Alastair Low, told the crowd: "I am sorry about the unsporting response which Paul Azinger's shot received at the 18th hole." Then, later, he said: "I cannot recall such rank bad sportsmanship. I thought it was disgraceful. This is not the way we expect spectators

to behave at an Open, even though it was such a small minority."

Azinger's 30 foot putt for the play-off was never in with a chance and suddenly Faldo was able to exult. At first he didn't. He cried. The emotion of the moment was too much for him, for he had achieved what he had set out to do in the world of golf, and it is given to few players of any sport to do that.

If that was a slightly unreal moment, then the whole day had a surreal air to it. The final round was played in what the Scots call a haar, a thick, clinging, clammy mist, through which golfers materialised from time to time and then passed away again, like ghosts. Azinger had led for most of the day, by three shots after five holes and by three again after eight. He had a good chance of making it four at the long 9th which was playing more like a par-four, but after deliberately laying up so that he could have an 80 yard sand wedge shot to the green – a distance he reckons he is deadly from – he hit a poor pitch and had to struggle for his five.

That was a minor turning point. But then Azinger dropped shots at the next two holes. The 10th was a hard hole, extracting fives from a large proportion of the field, but the 11th was one of the few birdie chances on the course. Azinger three putted it and suddenly the margin was down to one.

Up ahead, of course, Faldo was grinding out par after par. Somebody has probably had 18 pars in the final round of a championship before, but surely never to win the title. He had to hole from 7 feet for the one at the 11th, having left his second shot short, but there was a comforting air of reassurance about the Englishman as he went about the rest of his business.

He might have holed a 20-footer for a birdie at the short 16th but then Azinger had real chances, missing 10-footers at the 12th and 14th and a 15-footer at the 16th. Had any of those gone in it might have given the American the momentum, and the insurance he needed, for what was to happen to him at the final two holes. But there are many 'ifs' in a championship and all that matters at the end of the day is not so much what they were, as how you survived them. Nick Faldo, in the course of a week that had seen him survive not just the pressures but some of the most atrocious weather an Open has ever provided, had hit no more than two destructive drives, was in only one fairway bunker and had not three-putted, even once.

Golf of that calibre deserved a reward and it made Faldo into what the R&A call, oh so primly, the Champion Golfer for 1987. ●

The first of Faldo's final two putts on the 72nd hole.

Larry, Gayle, Drew and Josh Nelson with the USPGA trophy. He had won the same title in 1981.

THE U.S.P.G.A.

P.G.A. NATIONAL, PALM BEACH GARDEN, FLORIDA
6-9 AUGUST

People, like golf professionals and golf officials, like to pretend in the cause of diplomacy, that you cannot rank the majors. This is stuff and nonsense. The Open Championship is, like Wimbledon, the World Championship and is undoubtedly number one. The US Open, the championship of the strongest golfing country in the world, is number two. The US Masters is probably number three, because it is number one on the calendar, and the US PGA is number four. And no-one, as *Palm Beach County Sun-Sentinel* columnist, Steve Hummer, put it neatly, remembers the fourth kiss of a lifetime, the fourth man to walk on the moon.

The PGA's real, possibly only, claim to fame is as the fourth part of the 'Grand Slam', which in itself is a modern invention. You have only got to go back as far as 1953 to find that Ben Hogan, having won the Masters, US Open and Open Championship, chose not to play in the PGA that year because it was match-play and he did not think that his, by-then injured, legs would take the strain.

Having said all that it is nevertheless a major championship and most of the world's best players try to play in it. Not all of them are able to, because of the restrictions that hedge about all the US majors, although no fewer than 41 club professionals from the States played in this year's event.

A few, like Sandy Lyle, chose not to play because they did not fancy a week in Florida in August, and while that is nonsensical in terms of building a career, as a short-term consideration it made a great deal of sense. West Palm Beach was hot and humid. They have a thing called the 'temperature and humidity index' in the States, which is a formula for working out how hot if *feels*, as against what the thermometer registers. Every day it was over 100 degrees; it peaked at 115 and was twice at 111. It was no place to be playing a major championship. The reason they were, was political. The PGA of America have built their headquarters there and, obviously, their principal event has to be played on their golf course every now and again.

It was so hot that the PGA officials were reduced to being economical with the truth, both about the temperatures and the number of people who were prepared to brave it. The temperatures were in the nineties, according to them, and the attendance figures reached a total of 67,500. This, they admitted, was based on an estimate of the number of cars in the car park and the number of people who had travelled to the tournament in them. They said three per car; the universal formula is two per car, and in this part of wealthy America is more likely to be less than that. Suffice it to say that on the last day it was possible to watch the star three-ball of Ballesteros, Lanny Wadkins and Raymond Floyd without difficulty.

The weather also caused an outbreak of hats. Ian Woosnam wore a large straw boater, Bernhard Langer a stetson and Greg Norman an Australian outback creation called an Akubra (without the corks), modelled on the hat worn by Crocodile Dundee. In a practice round Jack Nicklaus took one look at it and said: "How much are they paying you for wearing that thing? They'd have to give me an awful lot of money."

There was also an outbreak of peevishness, concerning Norman. Paul Azinger dared to be honest about the Australian when some of Norman's comments were passed to him. Norman had said that all the world's top players these days were foreigners, to which Azinger replied: "I don't see how he can say that, he's only won four tournaments in six years." Of course, if that means American tournaments, Azinger is right, but Norman was upset. "This changes my perception of Paul," he said. "I'll be having a word with him about it."

More peevishness came from Nick Faldo. Three years ago in this championship he railed against the British press. This year, despite winning the Open and, hopefully having lost that particular chip from his shoulder, he used practically the same words and phrases. "They twist and turn your words," he said. "They sensationalize everything." The next morning he went off with his ghost writer to fulfil a contract for the *Daily Express*.

Two great players had trouble with the airlines before the Championship started. Hubert Green, despite taking his clubs to the check-in desk and seeing them tagged to the correct destination of his non-stop flight, nevertheless arrived there without the clubs – or his other luggage! "This is upsetting," he said with mas-

A very Australian hat for Greg Norman.

terly understatement. "I like to clean my teeth, comb my hair, play with the clubs I'm most comfortable with. When you're getting ready for a major this is not a good thing to happen." The clubs, which had started in Memphis, to go to Fort Lauderdale, turned up in San Francisco.

But even that was preferable to Tom Watson's experience. He left Kansas City on EA 323 and was but 12 minutes into the flight when the pilot announced that they were returning and warned the passengers to be ready for an emergency landing. An emergency light indicating an overheating part in the tail had come on, fire engines and rescue services lined the runway, and the passengers huddled into little balls behind the seat in front of them.

It was, thankfully, a faulty emergency light. They landed perfectly normally and Watson, very sincerely, said: "I'll never get nervous over a three foot putt again."

There was nostalgia too. Angelo Argea, who last caddied for Jack Nicklaus in 1981, emerged for one more effort. At 57 he found it hard work at first, but seeing them working together was like watching a re-run of an old video, and Argea survived the awful temperatures for all four rounds.

Tom Kite, a favourite with the crowds must wait another year to win a major.

Ian Woosnam collapsed to a first round 86, a great disappointment at his first tournament in America.

◆ INTO THE HEAT

The first day of the Championship saw even the trees looking for shade. The sun was relentless and there was time for the players to melt in it as rounds of golf took five or more hours to complete. "You could have hors d'oeuvre and dinner between swings," said the irrepressible Fuzzy Zoeller. Tom Watson said: "It's the hottest I've ever been on a golf course," while others were more picturesque. Rodger Davis: "It's stickier than Indonesia." Larry Nelson: "Like the rice paddy fields in Vietnam." Mac O'Grady (of course): "It's Tarzan's land out there."

In all, 32 players failed to break 80 and one of the worst was Ian Woosnam, who took 86. "I'm so embarrassed I'm going home," he said immediately after walking off the last green. Then, a few moments later, he decided that as an invited player it would be even more embarrassing to withdraw and he added, "in any case I can't even be bothered to lose my temper." Woosie was over-golfed and there was also an intriguing aspect to a part of his poor play.

He likes to play with irons that are three degrees flatter than standard because of his height, 5' 4½". But the clubs had worked themselves back to standard after being hammered flat. This had forced Woosnam's swing into a different and unwonted plane. He got them fixed after the first round and 75 for the second was a reasonable effort on the day.

Another player to perform badly on the first day was Paul Azinger, the leader of the US Money List at the time. He took 82 and proceeded to fracture the Queen's English as follows: "I didn't hit it unsolid. I just hit it 82 times." Unsolid?

There were some interesting, contrived partnerships. Arnold Palmer, age 57, played with Jack Nicklaus, 47, and Tom Watson, 37, and got the day's largest gallery. Roughly a dozen followed the three-ball of the current major Championship titleholders, Larry Mize,

Scott Simpson and Nick Faldo. Exactly 63 followed Zoeller, Norman and Hal Sutton. We know that because Norman counted, which says something about the numbers attending and the pace of play.

Bobby Wadkins led the championship with a four-under 68, David Edwards and club pro Fred Funk, the college coach at the University of Maryland, had 69's, but the danger seemed to lie among those on 70 – Curtis Strange, Bernhard Langer, Tom Watson, Raymond Floyd, Lanny Wadkins and Larry Nelson.

The greater danger came from soaring blood pressures for those spectators around the 18th green. There is an enormous raft moored in the lake that runs along the right side of the hole and on it a leader-board. There are red numbers to denote birdies, black numbers for pars and, on this first day, there was

LEADERS	HOLE	1	2
	PAR		
WADKINS B		1	1
WADKINS L		1	1
EDWARDS		3	3
STRANGE			
NELSON		2	2
FUNK		0	0
WATSON		1	2
COLE		1	0
LUMAN		0	1
LANGER		2	2

Scoreboard decoration.

An overall view.

also a green number. Her name was Danielle Cromb, aged 18.

She was a model from a local agency and had been hired by the PGA National golf club. She was rowed out to the raft, climbed aboard, took off her shirt and shorts and revealed a very small, very green, bikini. "Hi," she said, "they told me to sit out here and attract attention."

She certainly did that. Photographers flocked to the spot and later Colin Wright, President of the club was able to say, rightly, "It was the best publicity we had all day." But it was too much for the US PGA officials. Danielle was asked to leave and the girls booked for the succeeding days never even got on board.

◆ DAY TWO

Out went Ian Woosnam, whose Championship had hardly been the best advertisement for European golf. He left as leader of the Order of Merit, but it helped considerably that Paul Azinger, his American counterpart, also departed, only two shots better with rounds of 82 and 77 for 159. Larry Mize and Rodger Davis both took 156 and had to go home, while 16 shots ahead of them Floyd and Lanny Wadkins were in the lead. It was boiling up, literally and metaphorically, with Ballesteros, Crenshaw, Bobby Wadkins and Nelson all only two shots behind, and of all the contenders, perhaps Ballesteros was the favoured one. In one man's mind, the title was destined for the Spaniard.

He told him: "You can come to Florida like Ponce de Leon, one of your cousins from 400 years ago and you can find the Fountain of Youth. Your Fountain of Youth," he explained "is a major championship." Whether Ballesteros understood any of this is doubtful. Who said it? Why, Mac O'Grady of course.

Floyd, ever the realist, said: "I don't want any of that 'rah-rah' stuff. I've had an expletive-deleted year and there is a lot of golf yet to

Angelo Argea joins Jack Nicklaus as caddie
for the first time since 1981.

come," cautious words as befits a leader. Lanny Wadkins reminded the world that on the last two occasions when Floyd had won a major he had finished second and "it's time to turn that around."

Of the brothers Wadkins, Lanny and Bobby, it is the former who has won a major, the 1977 PGA, and the most money. Lanny is 38 to Bobby's 36, has won over 3 million dollars in 17 years on the pro tour to 1 million in 13 years by Bobby and said, when asked about both of them contending for a major title: "I don't mind Bobby being on the leader-board ... providing he's right behind me." Bobby, on the other hand, showed rather more brotherly love. "Neither of us lose," he said, "if Lanny wins. I'm his greatest fan."

Greg Norman mistakenly cleared his locker and gave the attendant a $30 tip, thinking that he had missed the cut. He then made plans for a few days in the Bahamas but, as more and more people found they could not cope with the rough, the qualifying score crept up and eventually the Australian was in, right on the mark.

But Jim Thorpe was not. Peter Thomson once said that all critical comments about a golf course should be surrounded not by the normal quotation marks but by the scores the player has just done. Hence: [65]This is the greatest course I've ever played.[65] Applying the same formula to Thorpe, it comes out like this: [79]They take a great course and they make the fairways 25 yards wide and they grow the rough. They got what they wanted alright.[75] After breaking his driver over his knee after

Arnold Palmer and defending champion Bob Tway both sported colonial hats to cope with the sun.

yet another errant drive at the 13th, he went home a disgruntled man.

◆ NEWCOMERS ON THE LEADER-BOARD

Fuzzy Zoeller, as ever, had a few words to say about it. "How" he demanded, "do you explain a DA Weibring?". After three rounds the scoreboard read: 212 DA Weibring,
M McCumber
213 R Floyd, B Wadkins

Zoeller went on: "DA hasn't done anything worth a damn all year and he suddenly finds a golf course he can play on." Zoeller was, of course, talking from the standpoint of 76, 71 and 76 and standing 11 shots behind the leader and with no hope of another major title. But it was a relevant question nonetheless, one which highlights the mysteries of form in golf. Weibring had five birdies, hit every fairway and was in his first challenging position of the year. He was 76th on the Money List at the time, had not been to a press room to explain his good play for a year or two and enjoyed, on this occasion, trotting out his favourite one-liner. It comes when, as inevitably happens, someone asks what the initials stand for: "Dont't Ask" is DA's standard reply. In fact they represent Donald Albert, after his father.

But if Zoeller found it hard to explain Weibring, how much more so Ballesteros explaining Ballesteros. "I'm trying to convince myself I'm a happy man," muttered the Spaniard, who was plainly anything but.

"If I had played good on the last four or five holes I could be three ahead." If he had been, not many people would have backed

---

The Wadkins brothers, Bobby and Lanny, and the Ballesteros brothers, Vicente and Severiano.

The wildlife of Florida, everything from herons to Golden Bears.

Vicente Ballesteros
with his Scotch
water bottle.

against him winning his fifth major, but instead he was two behind, having hit three totally uncharacteristic shots and visited the water twice. At the 15th he underclubbed, only just cleared the water hazard and had to hit one of his minor-miracle chips from the fluffy stuff to get his par. But at the 16th he leaked his tee shot to the right, it trickled into the pond that forms the corner of the dog-leg and that was a double-bogey six. Then he went for the really difficult shot that the second to the 18th represents if you are trying to make the green in two. "It was not the distance," said Ballesteros afterwards, who used a two-iron for the 220 yard shot, and got the required length. But the direction was awry, the ball splashed into the lake and that was a bogey six. The field heaved a collective sigh of relief and the Championship was wide open again.

One man who hoped to take advantage of these Spanish lapses was Mark McCumber, jointly in the lead with Don't Ask. He has had a solid enough career on the US Tour, with four victories and almost a million dollars in winnings, but has rarely been seen as a major championship winner. He confessed that he would be nervous on the first tee of the final round, but told a lovely little story of how he hoped to cope with the pressure.

When his daughter Addison was six he took her to a fun fair and they were queueing for one of the more frightening rides. They waited for almost two hours, in fact, and when the time eventually came to get on, Addison started crying.

McCumber said to her: "If you don't want to go, we don't have to." Addison replied: "Daddy, it's no fun if you're not scared."

McCumber was one of the few players to birdie the long 18th that day, and he did it after a long conference over the second shot with his caddie, local man Chico Fernandez. He had 249 yards to go, elected to hit a three-wood and "caught it right on the money. When

Both caddie and crowd found their own ways to keep cool.

Larry Nelson stayed cool enough to be leader in the clubhouse after 72 holes.

I got to the ball," said McCumber "we were both smiling." He got his birdie alright, but that shot could, just possibly, have cost him the title.

◆ THE ART OF STAYING COOL

He who chokes, if not last then certainly least, wins. Of the third round leaders – the men ahead of the winner – Raymond Floyd took 80, Severiano Ballesteros 78, Mark McCumber and Bobby Wadkins 77 and DA Weibring 76. Only one man remained in touch with respectability, Lanny Wadkins, with a one-over-par 73, good enough to get him into a play-off with Larry Nelson.

Their tying totals of 287 were the highest since stroke-play started in 1958, indicative of the brutal nature of the rough, the rest of the course and the weather.

The play-off was brief. Wadkins, because of his fiery match-play nature, started favourite, but both men missed the green of the 10th hole where the extra holes began. It is something of a lottery when your ball goes into the thick fringe grass around the putting surfaces, but both men drew reasonable lies and Nelson, chipping first, rolled his ball down to seven feet. Wadkins, with a slightly easier shot, got to five feet and then Nelson holed for a par.

"No-one was more surprised than me when Lanny missed," said Nelson afterwards. "Men-

Lanny Wadkins holes a four foot putt on the 18th for a play-off.

tally I had prepared to go to the next tee."

And so yet another member of the US Tour Bible Study Group, the 'God Squad' as they are irreverently and unoriginally known by their peers, had won yet another major.

The last four championships in the US, the 1986 PGA, the Masters, the US Open and now the PGA again had been won by Bob Tway, Larry Mize, Scott Simpson and Larry Nelson and the local papers were proclaiming them as the 'God Squad Grand Slammers'. It may, with a little heavenly foresight, have been predictable. After all, Nelson is one of the founder members of the Group and, as 'minister' he really had to keep pace with his 'congregation'. But perhaps his next sermon should be on humility, and addressed to himself.

After his win Nelson delivered himself of the following words: "I am proud to have won one of the great championships over one of the most difficult courses against one of the hardest fields beating one of the fiercest competitors there is." So there.

But Nelson had kept his head on a difficult day. In winning he had taken his third major championship, to add to his PGA victory in 1981 and his US Open in 1983 and had taken his lifetime winnings to $1,886,396. That took him ahead of Gary Player on the career winnings list, something that says more about inflation than respective abilities.

He had survived several challenges, not just that of Wadkins who, on the 18th, had elected not to go for the green in two but to rely on chipping and putting for a birdie, as he had done in the 1983 Ryder Cup. On that occasion he obtained the half point that made the Cup safe for America, and Jack Nicklaus kissed the divot dug up by Wadkins' wedge. This time Wadkins could only chip to 30 feet and had to hole from 4 feet for the play off.

But Scott Hoch could not only have been in that play-off, he had an extraordinary chance to win the Championship outright. He hit his third to 8 feet and, with a straightforward putt, went boldly for it. Had it gone in, he would

have been two-under and the likely winner. Instead it ran 3 feet past and now, with a putt to get into what would have been the play-off mark, Hoch suffered something of a brainstorm. "I had been concentrating so hard on the first putt, and it was such a shock when I missed it, that I gave no thought at all to the one back." He missed that, of course, and departed kicking himself.

Both Nelson and Wadkins were in the clubhouse by the time the last group played the last hole. Bobby Wadkins and Don't Ask were already out of contention but McCumber had an excellent chance of getting a birdie

Mark McCumber goes for it. His second shot on the 72nd hole with a driver from the fairway.

and joining the play-off. He had hit an excellent drive into the middle of the fairway and he and caddie Fernandez went into another protracted consultation. The fact that McCumber had hit the green with a three-wood in the third round weighed heavily in the negotiations and eventually a decision was reached. It was either, according to Larry Dorman of the *Miami Herald*: 'the gutsiest decision since Ollie North turned on the shredder, or the dumbest decision since Ollie North turned on the shredder.'

McCumber decided that, as the wind was a little more against than it had been on Satur-

day, if he wanted to reach the green in two – and he did – he would have to take his driver. He hit it well enough and the ball failed by only the tiniest of margins to stay dry. But 3 feet is 3 feet when the ball is in a lake, which is where McCumber deposited that second shot, and now his chance of an eagle and an outright win had totally vanished. He would have to hole a pitch shot for a birdie to get into the play-off. He actually got the ball to run almost over the hole with that approach,

Larry Nelson on the 71st hole.

The final scenes of the brief play-off, won by Nelson at the first extra hole.

Ben Crenshaw, the most consistent player in all four 1987 majors.

Ballesteros mops up after another frustrating championship. It was not his year.

but it stayed out and McCumber, in going for it all, had lost it all.

"Sure," he said afterwards, "people will second guess me and call me a fool. But if I'd hit it on the green and made eagle and won, then it would have been discussed a little, too."

If any one incident took the pressure off the leaders in the final round, it was the extraordinary eight taken by Ballesteros at the long 3rd. He stood on the tee as the leader of the Championship at three-under. He walked to the next tee in joint fourth position and was never to challenge again.

The hole featured at least three, and possibly four, bad shots, an argument with his brother and caddie, Vicente, followed by a shouting match with the same man. The hole encapsulated all that has been wrong with the Spaniard's golf in the major championships over the last few years.

The 3rd hole par 5 on the last day. Seve's fourth shot out of the rough into the bunker, his fifth shot over the green and into the lake. A penalty drop, a chip and a putt, all added up to a disastrous eight.

First of all he hit a bad tee shot, pulling it into the deep rough. He had no option but to chop it out some 20 yards onto the fairway. He then faced a very long shot, long whether to the green, or even if he wanted to lay up short. Vicente took out a club which looked like Seve's one-iron. Ballesteros clearly thought the two-iron would do. The two men argued the matter back and forth, eventually Seve prevailed and Vicente handed him the two-iron.

But Ballesteros cut it, short and right of the green, back in the three-inch-high rough. He exploded, perhaps forgetting that Spanish is a strong second language in Florida. There were plenty of spectators around to do the translating.

"Damelo o no me lo des," he said. "No me dudes."

Being translated this means, roughly: "Give it to me or don't, but whatever you do, don't doubt me." He was saying that Vicente's reluctance to give him the two-iron straight away had caused the bad shot, had planted the seed of doubt in his mind. But bad shot it was, as bad as the drive, and he then played another, fluffing the chip into a bunker in front of him.

Now a bogey six stared him in the face, assuming that, as one of the best bunker players in the world, he could get up and down in two. The ball lay well in the sand, he had plenty of green to work with, and yet he managed to thin the shot, skimming it over the green, full pitch into the crowd at the back and from there it trickled down into the edge of the lake. It was a terrible shot and now any score was possible for the hole. He had played five, a penalty drop made six and he still had a very tricky chip to get back onto the green.

In fact he played *that* shot superbly, to 10 feet, and holed the putt for an eight. Since the outburst on the fairway Ballesteros had been impassive, and he strode from the green completely deadpan. But in going from three-under to level-par he had not only destroyed his own chances, he had given every other contender breathing space. This time he was completely the architect of his own misfortunes and the constant complaint about bad luck – "nothing happens for me" – was simply not applicable in the 1987 USPGA Championship. ●

US MASTERS

$162,000	1	Larry Mize*	70727271	285
$79,200	2=	Seve Ballesteros	73717071	285
		Greg Norman	73746672	285
$37,200	4=	Ben Crenshaw	75706774	286
		Roger Maltbie	76667074	286
		Jodie Mudd	74727169	286
$26,200	7=	Jay Haas	72727273	289
		Bernhard Langer	71727076	289
		Jack Nicklaus	74727370	289
		Tom Watson	71727472	289
		D. A. Weibring	72757171	289
$17,640	12=	Chip Beck	75727073	290
		Tze-Chung Chen	74697176	290
		Mark McCumber	75716975	290
		Curtis Strange	71707376	290
		Lanny Wadkins	73727075	290
$13,050	17=	Paul Azinger	77736972	291
		M. Calcavecchia	73727868	291
		Sandy Lyle	77746872	291
		Craig Stadler	74747271	291
$10,800	21	Bobby Wadkins	76697374	292
$9,750	22=	Gary Koch	76755270	293
		Nick Price	73737176	293
$7,900	24=	John Cook	69737478	294
		Tom Kite	73747473	294
		Mark O'Meara	75747174	294
$6,267	27=	David Graham	73777273	295
		D. Hammond	73757473	295
		Corey Pavin	71718172	295
		Scott Simpson	72757276	295
		Denis Watson	76747372	295
		Fuzzy Zoeller	76717672	295
$5,200	33=	Calvin Peete	71777573	296
		Gene Sauers	75737474	296
$4,257	35=	Andy Bean	75697875	297
		Howard Clark	74717775	297
		Hubert Green	80717472	297
		John Mahaffey	73757673	297
		Gary Player	75757176	297
		Joey Sindelar	74708172	297
		Mark Wiebe	73747179	297
$3,333	42=	Johnny Miller	75757177	298
		Payne Stewart	71757478	298
		Jim Thorpe	77747671	298
$2,800	45=	David Frost	75707778	300
		Kenny Knox	75757575	300
		Don Pooley	76757673	300
$2,400	48	Mike Hulbert	76757179	301
$2,300	49	Bruce Lietzke	75747776	302
$2,200	50=	Tommy Aaron	72767681	305
		Dave Barr	79687979	305
		Billy Casper	77747579	305
		Mac O'Grady	72797975	305
Amateur	54	R. C. Lewis, Jr.	74777979	309

* Denotes won play-off

US OPEN

$150,000	1	Scott Simpson	71687068	277
$75,000	2	Tom Watson	72657170	278
$46,240	3	Seve Ballesteros	68756871	282
$24,543	4=	Bobby Wadkins	71717071	283
		Curtis Strange	71726971	283
		Bernhard Langer	69697372	283
		Ben Crenshaw	67727272	283
		Larry Mize	71687272	283
$15,004	9=	Dan Pohl	75716969	284
		Tommy Nakajima	68707472	284
		Mac O'Grady	71697272	284
		Jim Thorpe	70687373	284
		Lennie Clements	70707074	284
$12,065	14=	Bob Eastwood	73667571	285
		Isao Aoki	71737071	285
		Tim Simpson	76667073	285
$9,747	17=	M. Calcavecchia	73687372	286
		David Frost	70727173	286
		Jodie Mudd	72757168	286
		Jim Woodward	71747269	286
		Jumbo Ozaki	71697274	286
		Nick Price	69746974	286
		Kenny Knox	72716974	286
$7,720	24=	Don Pooley	74727269	287
		Jay Don Blake	70757171	287
		Steve Pate	71727272	287
		Craig Stadler	72687473	287
		Danny Edwards	72707273	287
		Peter Jacobsen	72717173	287
		John Mahaffey	72726776	287
$6,555	31=	Hal Sutton	74707074	288
		Tony Sills	71707572	288
		Ken Green	71747568	288
		Dale Douglass	70736976	288
		Keith Clearwater	74716479	288
$5,626	36=	Scott Hoch	72707770	289
		Sandy Lyle	70747273	289
		Lanny Wadkins	73717273	289
		Denis Watson	69747274	289
		Rodger Davis	75687274	289
		Barry Jaeckel	73707274	289
		John Cook	70687675	289
$4,857	43=	Sam Randolph	71717672	290
		Raymond Floyd	68737673	290
		Wayne Grady	73707473	290

FINAL SCORES

THE OPEN

$4,240	46=	Ralph Landrum	72717474	291
		Fred Couples	72717375	291
		Roger Maltbie	73737570	291
		Tom Kite	76697076	291
		Jack Nicklaus	70687677	291
$3,462	51=	Greg Norman	72697477	292
		Joey Sindelar	75717571	292
		David Hobby	77707372	292
		Gil Morgan	72717673	292
		David Graham	71767273	292
		Ed Dougherty	73677874	292
		Mark McCumber	72726979	292
$3,178	58=	Gene Sauers	72697379	293
		Bob Gilder	72727079	293
		Mark Wiebe	70677779	293
		Duffy Waldorf	74697575	293
		Bob Lohr	76677971	293
		Mike Smith	73717475	293
		Eddie King	73697576	293
		Jack Renner	73737176	293
$3,165	66=	Mark McNulty	73727376	294
		Russ Cochran	71698173	294
$3,165	68=	Tom Purtzer	74737771	295
		Jose-M. Olazabal	76697674	295
		Bob Tway	70717975	295
$3,165	71=	D. Hammond	75717674	296
		Jim Carter	75727574	296
$3,165	73	Gary Hallberg	71726985	297
$3,165	74	David Ogrin	74727478	298
$3,165	75=	D. Eichelberger	72757776	300
		Fred Wadsworth	75717777	300
$3,165	77	David Rummells	74737678	301

£75,000	1	Nick Faldo	68697171	279
£49,500	2=	Rodger Davis	64737469	280
		Paul Azinger	68687173	280
£31,000	4=	Ben Crenshaw	73687268	281
		Payne Stewart	71667272	281
£26,000	6	David Frost	70687074	282
£23,000	7	Tom Watson	69697174	283
£18,666	8=	Ian Woosnam	71697273	284
		Nick Price	68717273	284
		Craig Stadler	69697175	284
£13,500	11=	Mark McNulty	71697570	285
		Hal Sutton	71707371	285
		Jose-M. Olazabal	70737072	285
		Masashi Ozaki	69727173	285
		M. Calcavecchia	69707274	285
		Graham Marsh	69707274	285
£7,450	17=	Wayne Grady	70717669	286
		Sandy Lyle	76697170	286
		Eamonn Darcy	74697271	286
		Bernhard Langer	69697672	286
		Lee Trevino	67747372	286
		Mark Roe	74687272	286
		Ken Brown	69737074	286
		Raymond Floyd	72687076	286
£5,300	25	Gerard Taylor	69687575	287
£4,833	26=	David Feherty	74707767	288
		Gordon Brand Jnr	73707570	288
		Larry Mize	68717673	288
£4,200	29=	Lanny Wadkins	72717571	289
		Fuzzy Zoeller	71707672	289
		Ken Green	67767472	289
		Danny Edwards	71737273	289
		Anders Forsbrand	73697374	289
£3,900	34	David Graham	69737870	290
£3,500	35=	Ross Drummond	79667769	291
		Manuel Calero	71747571	291
		Jay Haas	69747672	291
		Greg Norman	71717475	291
		Bob Tway	67727577	291
£3,025	40=	Derrick Cooper	74727868	292
		Fred Couples	70747870	292
		Andy Bean	70737574	292
		Gordon Brand	72727474	292
£2,825	44=	Fulton Allem	74697773	293
		Brian Marchbank	72727673	293

		Ossie Moore	71727674	293
		Carl Mason	70697876	293
£2,675	48=	Larry Nelson	70757673	294
		John Slaughter	72717675	294
£2,525	50=	Mats Lanner	71747971	295
		Sam Torrance	76697773	295
		Seve Ballesteros	73707775	295
		Philip Walton	72737575	295
£2,350	54=	John O'Leary	71737973	296
		Roger Chapman	70737974	296
		Billy Andrade	74697875	296
£2,250	57=	Ove Sellberg	71727876	297
		Paul Mayo (A)	72707580	297
£2,150	59=	Brian Jones	73728073	298
		Bill McColl	71757775	298
		T. Nakajima	73727778	298
£1,975	62=	Scott Simpson	75718271	299
		Neil Hansen	75698075	299
		Howard Clark	72737876	299
		Miguel Martin	74717777	299
£1,750	66=	Mark O'Meara	73728273	300
		Gary Player	72747975	300
		Tateo Ozaki	72737877	300
		Hugh Baiocchi	72737877	300
		B. Chamblee	73727778	300
£1,600	71	Wayne Westner	71758471	301
£1,600	72=	Jack Nicklaus	74718176	302
		Tom Kite	73728176	302
£1,600	74	Jeff Hawkes	71748078	303
£1,600	75	Ricky Willison (A)	75718376	305
£1,600	76	Chris Moody	76708179	306
£1,600	77	David Jones	72748378	307
£1,600	78	Anthony Stevens	71758284	312

FINAL SCORES

US PGA

$150,000	1	Larry Nelson*	70727372	287			Bobby Cole	71747579	299
$90,000	2	Lanny Wadkins	70707473	287			Mac O'Grady	78707180	299
$58,750	3=	Scott Hoch	74747169	288	$2,400	47=	Tom Purtzer	75738171	300
		D. A. Weibring	73726776	288			D. Hammond	76747971	300
$37,500	5=	Mark McCumber	74696977	289			Fred Funk	69797973	300
		Don Pooley	73717372	289			Bob Betley	72797772	300
$27,500	7=	Ben Crenshaw	72707474	290			T. C. Chen	76757673	300
		Bobby Wadkins	68747177	290			Scott Simpson	78737673	300
$22,500	9	Curtis Strange	70767174	291			Tom Byrum	79727673	300
$17,000	10=	Seve Ballesteros	72707278	292			Bob Tway	78717675	300
		Nick Price	76717075	292			Mike Reid	71797476	300
		David Frost	75707176	292	$1,856	56=	Lonnie Nielsen	78737476	301
		Tom Kite	72777172	292			Hubert Green	74738074	301
$10,750	14=	Raymond Floyd	70707380	293			Morris Hatalsky	76757575	301
		Jeff Sluman	72697874	293			Chip Beck	75747280	301
		Dan Pohl	71787569	293			Mike Sullivan	73727482	301
		David Edwards	69757772	293	$1,740	61=	Steve Jones	72757481	302
		Tom Watson	70797371	293			Jim Woodward	79726982	302
		Curt Byrum	74756876	293			Steve Pate	76737677	302
$8,500	20	Peter Jacobsen	73757373	294	$1,700	64	Fuzzy Zoeller	76717680	303
$7,500	21=	Jim Hallet	73787371	295	$1,650	65=	John Mahaffey	77727780	306
		Bernhard Langer	70787770	295			Andy Bean	73787679	306
		Gil Morgan	75747076	295			Mark Wiebe	78737580	306
$5,975	24=	Gene Sauers	76746878	296			Arnold Palmer	76757976	306
		Jack Nicklaus	76737473	296	$1,600	69	Ray Freeman	71777485	307
		Payne Stewart	72757574	296	$1,600	70	Greg Norman	73787979	309
		Ken Brown	73747376	296	$1,600	71	Lindy Miller	73788278	311
$4,383	28=	Bobby Clampett	71727777	297	$1,600	72	John Jackson Jr.	77748478	313
		John Cook	76707279	297	$1,600	73	Lon Hinkle	74767989	318
		Russ Cochran	73766979	297			Mark McNulty	737375	WD
		Jay Haas	74707677	297					
		Craig Stadler	75727575	297	* Denotes won play-off				
		Ronnie Black	76707675	297					
		Hal Sutton	73747476	297					
		Roger Maltbie	74727576	297					
		Chris Perry	75757473	297					
		Bruce Lietzke	75767472	297					
		Nick Faldo	73737774	297					
		Brad Fabel	73737774	297					
$3,400	40=	Robert Wrenn	75727675	298					
		Phil Blackmar	74728072	298					
		Denis Watson	76757275	298					
$3,050	43=	Tim Simpson	71708177	299					
		Buddy Gardner	75747971	299					